Twayne's English Authors Series

EDITOR OF THIS VOLUME

Bertram Davis

Florida State University

James Thomson

James Thomson

JAMES THOMSON

By HILBERT H. CAMPBELL

Virginia Polytechnic Institute and State University

TWAYNE PUBLISHERS

A DIVISION OF G. K. HALL & CO., BOSTON

Published in 1979 by Twayne Publishers,
A Division of G. K. Hall & Co.

Printed on permanent/durable acid-free paper and bound
in the United States of America

First Printing

Frontispiece portrait by William Aikman courtesy of
the Huntington Library.

Library of Congress Cataloging in Publication Data
Campbell, Hilbert H
James Thomson.

(Twayne's English authors series; TEAS 269)
Bibliography: p. 166–72
Includes index.
1. Thomson, James, 1700–1748.
2. Poets, Scottish—18th Century—Biography. I. Title.
PR3733.C3 821'.5 79-2508
ISBN 0-8057-6715-0

For Pat, Greg, and David

Contents

About the Author

Hilbert H. Campbell was born in West Virginia in 1934 and now lives in Blacksburg, Virginia, with his wife and two sons. He received the B.A. in 1958 and the M.A. in 1960 from Marshall University in Huntington, West Virginia. He was the recipient of a Danforth Teacher Grant for the years 1963-66, and he received the Ph.D. degree from the University of Kentucky in 1966. He is now professor of English at Virginia Polytechnic Institute and State University, Blacksburg, Virginia.

Campbell's main area of scholarly interest is eighteenth-century English literature, with a special interest in Joseph Addison, James Thomson, and Samuel Johnson. He has published scholarly studies focusing on these writers in *Philological Quarterly, Modern Philology, Studies in English Literature, 1500–1900, Texas Studies in Literature and Language, Bulletin of Bibliography, English Language Notes, Notes and Queries,* and *American Notes and Queries.* He has also written several substantial reviews for *Papers of the Bibliographical Society of America.* Among these are included extensive review essays analyzing studies or bibliographies of Laurence Sterne, Horace Walpole, Humfrey Wanley, and Jonathan Swift.

Campbell's substantial annotated bibliography of James Thomson scholarship from the eighteenth through the twentieth century was published by Garland Publishing, Inc. of New York. He is also coeditor of a volume of essays on Sherwood Anderson, published by Whitston Publishing Company of Troy, New York, in 1976.

Preface

My aim in this study is to provide a critical account of the poetic and dramatic career of the eighteenth-century poet James Thomson (1700–1748). Douglas Grant's biography of Thomson and several specialized studies of *The Seasons* are available to students; but no study attempting a comprehensive critical account of Thomson's work has appeared since G. C. Macaulay's volume in the English Men of Letters series in 1908. The inclusion of Thomson in the Twayne series provides an opportunity not only to incorporate new information which has become available since Macaulay's time, but also to make use of the much more sensible perspective on Thomson's career and accomplishment which has prevailed only in fairly recent critical discussions.

Most importantly, it is necessary to repudiate or at least modify a long tradition of criticism which assumed that Thomson was a complete anomaly in his own period. Influential critics of the nineteenth and early twentieth centuries, who never tired of condemning neoclassicism and praising romanticism, simply moved Thomson out of the Augustan period. In 1903, for example, Edmund Gosse remarked of *The Seasons* that "in spirit, in temper, in style, it has nothing whatever to do with that age, but inaugurates another, which, if we consider exactly, culminated, after a slow but direct ascent, in Wordsworth."[1] In this persistent and absurdly one-sided critical tradition, Thomson's accomplishments, virtues, and faults were all measured by the yardstick of how well or how poorly he managed to foreshadow Wordsworth. On the other hand, the conviction on which I have based my analyses in this study is that the nature and significance of not only Thomson's accomplishments but also his failures can be grasped only by placing him squarely in the context of his backgrounds, ambitions, and purposes as an Augustan writer. In no other way does his career make sense.

Chapter 1 will be chronologically arranged, following Thomson's life from 1700 to 1748, but with constant emphasis on the personal, social, and political factors which largely account for the pattern of his literary career and for the kind of literary distinction he achieved or failed to achieve. Chapter 2 deals with important aspects of Thomson's major poem *The Seasons*, including backgrounds, themes, structure, style, and revisions. Chapter 3 takes up Thomson's ambitious political poem *Liberty*, other political poems, and the five classical tragedies which he wrote for the London stage. Chapter 4 discusses *The Castle of Indolence* and some of Thomson's love poems and elegies. Chapter 5 is devoted to a brief account of Thomson's extensive influence and reputation.

For their hospitality and for aid in preparing this study, I am grateful to the Virginia Polytechnic Institute and State University Library, Harvard University Library, Yale University Library, the University of Virginia Library, Duke University Library, and the Library of Congress. My wife, Patricia Fannin Campbell, has helped me in more ways than I have space to acknowledge.

HILBERT H. CAMPBELL

Virginia Polytechnic Institute and State University

Chronology

1700 James Thomson born at Ednam, Roxburghshire, September 11 (old style), son of Thomas Thomson, Presbyterian minister, and Beatrix Trotter Thomson.

ca. 1712–1714 Attends a grammar school kept in the aisle of Jedburgh Church; writes juvenile verse.

1715 Matriculates at the College of Edinburgh.

1720 Contributes three poems: "Of A Country Life," "Upon Happiness," and "Verses on Receiving a Flower from His Mistress" to *The Edinburgh Miscellany.*

1724 August 28, publishes poem, "The Works and Wonders of Almighty Power," in Aaron Hill's London periodical *The Plain Dealer.*

1725 Late February, leaves Scotland for London.

1726 Late March, publishes *Winter.*

1727 February, *Summer;* May 8, *A Poem Sacred to the Memory of Sir Isaac Newton.*

1728 June, *Spring.*

1729 January 21, publishes *Britannia* anonymously; April, publishes four poems, "Hymn on Solitude," "The Happy Man," "A Paraphrase on the Latter Part of the VIth Chapter of St. Matthew," and "The Incomparable Soporific Doctor" in James Ralph's *Miscellaneous Poems by Several Hands.*

1730 February 28, *Sophonisba,* Thomson's first tragedy, acted at Drury Lane. June, *The Seasons,* including for the first time *Autumn* and "A Hymn on the Seasons." November, goes abroad and remains in Europe until late 1732 or early 1733.

1735 Three parts of *Liberty:* January 13, "Antient and Modern Italy Compared"; February 7, "Greece"; March 24, "Rome."

1736 Fourth and fifth parts of *Liberty* published: mid-January, "Britain"; mid-February, "The Prospect."

1737	June, *Poem to the Memory of the Right Honourable the Lord Talbot.*
1738	April 6, *Agamemnon* acted at Drury Lane.
1739	March 26, *Edward and Eleonora* "forbid to be acted" for political reasons.
1740	August 1, Thomson and Mallet's *Alfred: A Masque,* containing "Rule, Britannia" privately produced at Clive-don.
1744	Extensively revised and expanded edition of *The Seasons.*
1745	March 18, *Tancred and Sigismunda* acted at Drury Lane.
1748	May 7, *The Castle of Indolence*. Thomson dies August 27.
1749	January 13, *Coriolanus* acted at Covent Garden.

CHAPTER 1

A Poet's Career, 1700–1748

THE watershed year of James Thomson's life was 1725. In February of that year, when he was twenty-four, he embarked at Leith for London, never to return to Scotland. Destined at home to follow his father into the austere and impoverished Presbyterian clergy, he escaped to London and soon took his place among the hordes who aspired to make a living by the pen. The "high road to London" was a prospect which appealed to many Scots after the Act of Union brought the Kingdom of Great Britain into being in 1707. More fortunate than most, Thomson successfully established himself as a writer with the publication of *Winter* in 1726. He soon gave up the idea of pursuing the ministry, in Scotland or in England, and was thereafter "the poet Thomson," or "Mr. Thomson, Author of *The Seasons*," and later "the celebrated Mr. Thomson." He never married; and he lived comfortably if not affluently from the sale of his poetry, the production and sale of his plays, and pensions and sinecures provided by his patrons. Liberal in his thinking, genial and self-indulgent, he died a premature death in 1748 with the honest esteem of his friends, a rising reputation, and 237 bottles of wine and ale left over in the cellar of his house in Kew-Lane, Richmond. To imagine this pliable and genial man presiding over a stern Presbyterian manse in eighteenth-century Scotland is difficult. William Howitt, an 1847 visitor to Ednam, Thomson's birthplace, attended services in the church and was astonished by "*two* enormously long sermons, three prayers, three singings, and, to make worse of it, the sermons consisted of such a mass of doctrinal stubble as filled me with astonishment. . . ." Of the Scottish clergy, the same visitor thought that "Perhaps no class of people have less of the poetical or the picturesque in them than the Presbyterian clergy of Scotland."[1] The church in Roxburghshire must have been bleak and doctrine-ridden indeed in Thomson's day; for Howitt's observations were made a century later—a century usually supposed to have been characterized by liberalization and intellectual growth in Scotland. Thomson, of whom Dr. Johnson said that he had "the power of viewing everything in a poetical light,"[2] almost certainly avoided an uncongenial existence when he boarded the ship for London in 1725.

I *Early Career in Scotland, 1700–1725*

Thomson was born in the Border village of Ednam, Roxburghshire, September 11, 1700 (old style). A child of the Presbyterian manse, he was the fourth of nine children born to the Reverend Thomas Thomson and Beatrix Trotter Thomson. Before the future poet was two months old, the family moved to Southdean, near Jedburgh, on November 6, 1700. Thomson spent the first fifteen years of his life in the Presbyterian manse of this rural and isolated parish. The poet's father, although only the son of a gardener, had been educated for the ministry at the College in Edinburgh[3] and was reported to be "highly respected . . . for his piety, and his diligence in the pastoral duty." His mother was "a person of uncommon natural endowments; possessed of every social and domestic virtue; with an imagination, for vivacity and warmth, scarce inferior to her son's. . . ."[4] Thomson's boyhood home life, although little is known of it, must have been happy; for, in the last year of his life, he referred easily to his father and mother as "good and tender-hearted Parents" and expressed regret that they "did not live to receive any material Testimonies of that highest human Gratitude I owed them."[5]

In addition to a happy home life, the chief influences from this period on Thomson's future poetry must have been the pervasive religious atmosphere and the awesome natural setting in which he spent his formative years. The first of these, the religious influence, takes a rather interesting form. For the exceedingly stern and dogma-ridden Scotch Presbyterianism of the era found but shallow soil for nurture in the amiable and "poetical" temperament of James Thomson. More likely, as Patrick Murdoch, Thomson's close friend and biographer, speculates, "his early acquaintance with the sacred writings contributed greatly to that *sublime,* by which his works will be for ever distinguished."[6] For it was the Book of Job, "crowned with a description of the grand works of Nature; and that, too, from the mouth of their Almighty Author,"[7] which seized his imagination. Even more than Job, the Psalms—with their ecstatic praise of God seen in his creation—provided a chief impulse for the later "majestic freedom" and "grand images"[8] of *The Seasons.*

The harshness, beauty, and stark contrast of the seasons in Thomson's boyhood home also influenced his imagination in a profound way. A detailed and vivid firsthand description of the Southdean area was given in 1951 by the late Douglas Grant, who relates it specifically to Thomson's later portrayal of landscapes in poetry:

There stretches to the south of Southdean the great barren range of the Cheviots. . . . A desolate region, whose tufted marshes and spongy hillocks are threaded by a network of streams which make their way down through rocky channels into the glens. . . . When Thomson . . . stood upon the high places about his home, and turned his back to the hills, he would see laid out before him the long sweep of a delightful pastoral landscape. . . . The eye moves down along a valley, follows it until it widens and enters another, and continues on across a plain which is bounded only by the horizon. This landscape is ordered into foreground, middle distance, and distance, as deliberately as though it had been arranged by some great seventeenth-century artist, a Salvator Rosa or a Gaspar Poussin. . . . From the heights the volatile interchange of sunlight and shadow can be followed across the plain. . . . Each change of wind or weather is finely and immediately recorded in the variations of light.[9]

Thomson later on came under other and more sophisticated influences, but these early impressions remain perhaps the most important. For if Thomson did bring something "new" to English poetry, as has so often been proclaimed, it was a practiced eye and appreciation for the manifold manifestations of nature which he imbibed early and never lost while spending most of his life in Edinburgh and London. His poetic vision was later colored and complicated by a whole range of other interests and influences, but the fact that he began life where he did remains basic to an understanding of his poetry. The power of this passage in *Winter* results from a firsthand acquaintance with "the grand works of Nature":

At last the roused-up river pours along:
Resistless, roaring, dreadful, down it comes,
From the rude mountain and the mossy wild,
Tumbling through rocks abrupt, and sounding far;
Then o'er the sanded valley floating spreads,
Calm, sluggish, silent; till again, constrained
Between two meeting hills, it bursts a way
Where rocks and woods o'erhang the turbid stream;
There, gathering triple force, rapid and deep,
It boils, and wheels, and foams, and thunders through.

(ll. 96–105)

Immediately following these lines, the poet enthusiastically calls attention to the "sublime" in nature, a sense of which he had imbibed from his surroundings in youth:

> Nature! great parent! whose unceasing hand
> Rolls round the Seasons of the changeful year,
> How mighty, how majestic are thy works!
> With what a pleasing dread they swell the soul,
> That sees astonished, and astonished sings!
>
> (ll. 106–10)[10]

Both of Thomson's early biographers, Robert Shiels (1753) and Patrick Murdoch (1762), stress the formative influence of Robert Riccaltoun, a young farmer in Thomson's neighborhood, on the future poet. Riccaltoun is described by Murdoch as "a man of uncommon penetration and good taste"[11] and by Shiels as "a man of such amazing powers, that many persons of genius . . . have been astonished [at his] great merit."[12] The young Thomson found in Riccaltoun a kindred spirit and a lasting influence, a man who like himself was distinguished, according to Riccaltoun's friend Dr. Somerville, by "a benevolent heart, a rich imagination, a taste for what was beautiful and sublime in the works of nature."[13] We have Thomson's own testimony that "Mr. Rickleton's poem on winter, which I still have, first put the design [of *Winter*] into my head. In it are some masterly strokes that awaken'd me."[14] Riccaltoun later told Somerville that "a poem of his own composition, . . . the description of a storm or the effects of an extraordinary fall of snow on the hill of Ruberslaw, suggested to Thomson the idea of expatiating on the same theme, and produced the divine poem of his *Winter*."[15]

Thomson's more formal education took place at first in a grammar school kept in the aisle of Jedburgh Church, where he was drilled in the Latin exercises which were then the backbone of Scottish education and which later on influenced the style and vocabulary of his poetry so noticeably. In 1715 he matriculated at the College of Edinburgh. After his father's death on February 9, 1716, his mother moved her large family to Edinburgh, "where she lived in a decent frugal manner" and provided a home and family for "her favourite son."[16] Thomson's remaining in the bosom of his family until nearly age twenty-five gave him a lasting affection for the memory of his parents and an abiding concern for the welfare of his brothers and sisters, particularly the three youngest, Elizabeth, Jean, and John, whom he continued to befriend long after he had established himself in London. Thomson had apparently mastered his Latin at Jedburgh; for at Edinburgh he passed over the class of the professor of humanity (restricted to Latin) and matriculated at once in the Greek class, usually the second year of the Arts curriculum.[17] After Greek, Thomson progressed through logic, the normal third-year course, and natural philosophy, which in most instances conducted the student to his degree. About 1719, "His course of attendance upon the classes of philosophy being finished, he was entered in the Divinity Hall, as one of the candidates for the ministry, where the students, before they are permitted to enter on their probation, must yield six years attendance."[18] Thomson pursued seriously his divinity studies, and the records show that he delivered prescribed lectures in 1720, 1722, 1723, and 1724. He even received financial assistance from the presbytery at Jedburgh in the form of a bursary beginning in November, 1720, which continued until the end of 1724.[19] Both Thomson and the Presbyterian ministers who assisted him at this time must have fully expected that his talents and future efforts would belong to the church.

Thomson in later life was an intellectual liberal in both the ideas and forms of his poetry; and the winds of change which were beginning to blow both in the college and in the city during his residence in Edinburgh helped determine the direction of his development. Beginning about 1708, the College of Edinburgh reformed itself on the model of "the most famous Universities abroad," particularly Utrecht and Leyden. The utilization of a professor to teach only one specialized subject proved much more efficient than the older "Regenting" system, a rigid and antiquated arrangement whereby one man conducted his own pupils through all stages of the arts curriculum. Other old habits were also being discarded, the most important being the interpretation of "natural philosophy" as synonymous with Aristotle. Robert Stewart, who had been appointed professor of natural philosophy in 1708, and who conducted Thomson through the last year of the arts curriculum, was at least partially a Newtonian.[20] The influence of Newton and the whole complex of new scientific and philosophical notions associated with his outlook had been influential at Edinburgh as early as 1683;[21] and this particular aspect of the intellectual climate in which Thomson was nurtured from 1715 to 1725 is extremely important in understanding his later inclination to absorb into his work the latest and most liberal developments in science, philosophy, and theology.

What Alexander Grant calls "the extraordinary process of development" in the College of Edinburgh after 1708 was made possible in part by a period of relative stability following the Act of Union in 1707. The Union probably also served to stimulate the remarkable interest in English writers which developed in Scotland about the time of Thomson's residence in Edinburgh. Douglas Grant has rightly estimated that the literary clubs and societies which were formed at this time to study and imitate the best English authors were of greater significance to Thomson's development than his official education.[22] Patrick Murdoch, who was at Edinburgh with Thomson, remarks on this development: "About this time, the study of poetry was become general in *Scotland,* the best *English* authors being universally read, and imitations of them attempted. *Addison* had lately displayed the beauties of *Milton's* immortal work; and his remarks on it, together with Mr. *Pope's* celebrated *Essay,* had opened the way to an acquaintance with the best poets and critics."[23] Thomson participated in the activities of the literary societies and published three poems in the *Edinburgh Miscellany* in 1720. According to David Mallet, Thomson was at the time looked upon as "that dull fellow" and "the jest of our club."[24] This is hardly surprising, for Thomson's early verses are undistinguished and show little promise of the distinction which he was later to achieve as a poet. Thomson and his contemporaries "spoke and thought in broad Scots";[25] and their first carefully cultivated attempts to imitate the best English authors were awkward, artificial, and "literary." Indeed, Thomson's vocabulary and style remained to the end highly Latinized—a feature entirely natural for a Scot of the period[26]—rhetorical, and strongly flavored by literary, as opposed to natural, speech and allusion. At this time Thomson studied Addison, Pope, Gay, and other writers of the contemporary scene; but the English authors who eventually fired his imagination most and inspired him to emulation were Milton, Spenser, and Shakespeare. Along with the Old Testament and Virgil, the major literary influences on Thomson were Milton and Spenser. According to his first biographer Shiels, "He is indeed the eldest born of Spenser, and he has often confessed that if he had anything excellent in poetry, he owed it to the inspiration he first received from reading the Fairy Queen, in the very early part of his life."[27] Thomson in his mature work neglected what Murdoch calls "satirical or epigrammatic wit, a smart *antithesis* richly trimmed with rhime,"[28] or what Thomson himself calls "little glittering prettinesses, mixed turns of wit and expression" in favor of the more "sublime" strains, which had, again in his own words, "charmed the listening world from Moses down to Milton."[29]

Thomson's early poems, or the portion of them which survive in manuscript or published form, foreshadow in some ways the subject matter of *The Seasons;* but they are very unlike his later work in form and mastery of technique. Thomson's efforts at poetry prior to the publication of *Winter* in March, 1726, are known to us from three main sources: (1) A surviving holograph manuscript containing twenty-nine poems or fragments dating perhaps from the period 1716–1719; (2) Three poems: "Of a Country Life," "Upon Happiness," and "Verses on Receiving a Flower from His Mistress," published in *The Edinburgh Miscellany* in 1720; and (3) A poem, "The Works and Wonders of Almighty Power," published in Aaron Hill's London periodical *The Plain Dealer* on August 28, 1724. Each of the three deserves brief consideration in an account of Thomson's career and development.

The manuscript, which has on its title page, not in Thomson's hand, "Juvenile Poems wrote by James Thomson Author of the Seasons at the Age of [figure deleted] Years," was first brought to public attention in 1818 when a young London bookseller named William Goodhugh had possession of it.[30] Goodhugh also discussed and quoted from the manuscript in his *The English Gentleman's Library Manual* (London, 1827). After extensive travels, this interesting and important document found its way to the Newberry Library in Chicago in 1890; it has been exhaustively discussed and described in two excellent articles by H. Schmidt-Wartenberg and Alan D. McKillop.[31] The twenty-nine poems represent a large variety of "juvenile" experiments, but can be grouped roughly as follows: six pastorals, six lover's addresses to women or their beauty, five religious poems or paraphrases, three fables, three "descriptive" poems, one erotic poem, one poetical epistle, one satire on feminine fashion, one town description, one song, and one elegy. As other critics have remarked, these poems show no distinction and little promise. Thomson's later extensive religious and didactic interests are here foreshadowed, and also his inclination to descriptive poetry. In these early poems, however, there are more echoes of Addison, Pope, Gay, Sir Richard Blackmore, Allan Ramsay, and other contemporary writers than of his later and more fruitful models Milton and Spenser. Also, Thomson had not yet found his true métier of blank verse; twenty-two of the poems are written in couplets, the remainder in rhyming stanza forms. Even in his early paraphrases of the Psalms, which remained for him a great source of inspiration in *The Seasons,* the results are flat and disappointing. He took the majesty and simplicity of "O LORD, how manifold are thy works! in wisdom hast thou made them all: the earth is full of thy riches" (Psalm 104:24) and turned it into

> How many are thy wondrous works, O Lord!
> They of thy wisdom solid proofs afford:
> Out of thy boundless goodness thou didst fill,
> With riches and delights, both vale and hill.[32]

Thomson never did manage the simplicity of the Psalms, but later in *The Seasons* he came much closer to their dignity and nobility than in this early lifeless paraphrase. In descriptive passages also, the Thomson of *The Seasons* is not recognizable in these weakly conventional early lines:

> Pomona makes the trees with fruit abound,
> And blushing Flora paints the enamelled ground.
> . . . .
> O'er the fair landscape sportive zephyrs scud,
> And by kind force display the infant bud.
> The vegetable kind here rear their head,
> By kindly showers and heaven's indulgence fed.[33]

Two of the manuscript poems, "Verses on Receiving a Flower from His Mistress" and "Upon Happiness," were published in *The Edinburgh Miscellany* in 1720 in more polished versions. "Upon Happiness" is a dream vision in which the poet views from the mountain of Contemplation the vain pursuits after worldly felicity and encourages pursuit of virtue and religion. The poem is conventional and is derived specifically from Thomson's reading of John Norris and Sir Richard Blackmore. The third poem contributed to *The Edinburgh Miscellany* was "Of A Country Life," which is more interesting than anything Thomson had written before. Despite its stiff monotonous couplets and awkward diction, it includes some material which Thomson later altered or expanded for use in *The Seasons.* The "delightful prospects" of each season in the country are reviewed briefly; and the coming of winter as described in *The Seasons* is particularly foreshadowed in this passage:

Anon black Winter, from the frozen north,
Its treasuries of snow and hail pours forth;
Then stormy winds blow through the hazy sky;
In desolation nature seems to lie;
The unstained snow from the full clouds descends,
Whose sparkling lustre open eyes offends.
In maiden white the glittering fields do shine;
Then bleating flocks for want of food repine,
With withered eyes they see all snow around,
And with their fore feet paw, and scrape the ground.[34]

Passages in the poem on the "sweet and innocent . . . country sports" of fishing and hunting were later altered and expanded for inclusion in *Spring* and *Autumn* respectively, although neither sport is later represented as entirely "sweet and innocent." In fact, hunting in *Autumn* is presented as a "falsely cheerful barbarous game of death" (l. 384). As A. D. McKillop has pointed out,[35] "Of A Country Life" is an imitation of John Gay's *Rural Sports,* which first appeared in 1713 and in revised form in 1720.

Thomson's next publication, "The Works and Wonders of Almighty Power," a blank verse paraphrase of passages from Shaftesbury's *Moralists,* appeared in Aaron Hill's London periodical *The Plain Dealer* on August 28, 1724. The poem is interesting not only in foreshadowing Thomson's characteristic use of blank verse and the significant influence of Shaftesbury on *The Seasons,* but also as the first link between Thomson and the literary world of London. Aaron Hill, a prominent patron and the center of a literary coterie in London during the 1720s, had taken an interest in the new Edinburgh literary clubs and was by 1724 sponsoring the literary efforts of two of Thomson's Scotch acquaintances who had preceded him to London, Joseph Mitchell and David Mallet. Hill printed Thomson's poem to show how learning was flourishing in Edinburgh and introduced it enthusiastically:

To how surprising a Degree these fine Spirits have succeeded, in their noble *End,* let the following Sentiments declare; conceiv'd, and express'd, with all the Clearness, Depth, and Strength, of an *experienc'd Philosopher,* by a Member of this *Grotesque Club,* who was in his *Fourteenth Year only,* when he compos'd, in Blank Verse, a Poem, now in my Hands; and founded on a Supposition of the Author's sitting, a whole Summer Night, in a Garden, looking upward, and quite losing himself, in Contemplation on *the Works, and Wonders, of Almighty Power.*—If this was a Subject, naturally above the Capacity of so very a Boy, to what a Degree does it increase our Wonder, when we find it treated, in this Masterly Manner![36]

It is not surprising that Thomson's first literary connections when he later came to London were with Hill's circle.

II *London and the Grand Tour, 1725–1733*

What exactly did Thomson have in mind when he left Edinburgh for London in 1725? Both Shiels and Murdoch give the impression that he "had dropt all thoughts of the clerical profession"[37] before leaving Edinburgh, partly because of a rebuke given him by William Hamilton, the divinity professor, and went to London with the express design of trying his literary fortunes. But he wrote to his friend William Cranstoun after arriving in London that "I firmly resolve to pursue divinity as the only thing now I am fitt for"; and references in his letters to "the great design of my coming hither" and to "the business you know I design"[38] remain somewhat cryptic. Thomson's biographers have interpreted the evidence variously, and no certain answer is likely to be found. Thomson did have literary inclinations and ambitions in which he had been encouraged; and he probably followed Mitchell and Mallet to London under the impulse of these ambitions. He admitted to Cranstoun when he left Edinburgh that he had not "fix'd on any particular view";[39] and he retained the nagging conviction, which seems to have been much on his mind during his first six months in England, that he was destined to return to Scotland and the ministry. That a certain amount of impulsiveness and uncertainty characterize Thomson's move to London is not surprising. Bewildered by the metropolis, beset by homesickness, saddened by news of his mother's death three months after his departure, and disappointed in the employment he was able to find teaching a five year old child to read ("a low task you know not so suitable to my temper"), he reflected on the relative security of returning to "my original Study of Divinity; for, you know the business of a Tutor is only precarious, and for the present."[40] But Thomson's inclinations toward the ministry could not by this time have been very strong, and he soon was occupied fully with plans to make his way in London.

A large number of Thomson's fellow countrymen were by this time living in London; and it was to prominent Scotsmen that Thomson first carried his letters of introduction in 1725. He gained some assistance from Duncan Forbes of Culloden, at the time representing Inverness in Parliament and later lord president of the Court of Session. Forbes introduced him to others who could help him, including William Aikman the painter, whose death in 1731 Thomson remembered with a poignant elegy. David Mallet, his schoolfellow, was living in London as a tutor in the family of the duke of Montrose and provided him invaluable assistance and companionship during his early years in London. Although Thomson fairly soon broadened his circle of acquaintance and his base of support, he was heavily dependent during the first few years in London on his fellow Scots, who provided him employment, published his poems and purchased them, and brought their "tuneful Hands and merry Feet" to the theater to support his first play.[41] The preponderance of Scots in the subscription list for the 1730 collected *Seasons*—including Duncan Forbes (five copies), the provost of Edinburgh (ten copies), and the Edinburgh bookseller Gavin Hamilton (four copies)—shows something of the solidarity with which Thomson was patriotically supported by his countrymen.

A letter written in early October, 1725, from Thomson at East Barnet to his friend William Cranstoun in Scotland shows the poet at work on *Winter:* "Nature delights me in every form, I am just now painting her in her most lugubrious dress; for my own amusement, describing winter as it presents it self."[42] Thomson wrote his best nature poetry, and particularly *Winter,* with the grand scenery of his boyhood home vivid in his mind's eye. He writes to Cranstoun:

> Now, I imagine you seized w^{t} a fine romantic kind of a melancholy, on the fading of the Year. Now I figure you wandering, philosophical, and pensive, amidst the brown, wither'd groves: while the leaves rustle under your feet.
>
> The sun gives a farewell parting gleam and the birds
> Stir the faint note, and but attempt to sing.
>
> then again, when the heavns wear a more gloomy aspect, the winds whistle and the waters spout. I see you in the well known Cleugh, beneath the solemn Arch of tall, thick embowring trees, listning to the amusing lull of the many steep, moss grown Cascades, while deep, divine Contemplation, the genius of the place, prompts each swelling awfull thought. I'm sure you would not resign your part in that scene att an easy rate. none e'er enjoy'd it to the height you do, and you're worthy of it. ther I walk in spirit, and disport in its beloved gloom. this country, I am in. is not very entertaining. no variety but that of woods, and them we have in abundance. but where is the living stream? the airy mountain? and the hanging rock? with twenty other things that elegantly please the lover of nature?[43]

Undoubtedly *Winter,* which a homesick Thomson wrote shortly after his arrival in England, shows more impact of the Border scenery than the later poems, but his early impressions remained strong.

Winter was published in late March, 1726, by John Millan, a young Scots bookseller just then establishing himself in London. Thomson's earlier verse had been uniformly undistinguished; and the power of this 405 line poem, which by 1746 was to be expanded to 1069 lines, comes as something of a surprise. The poem aroused interest far beyond what might have been expected from the first brief effort of a completely unknown writer. In a long laudatory review in the *London Journal,* June 4, 1726, the reviewer remarks: "Whoever this Gentleman be, whose Name is prefixed to this Poem, whether a real or a fictitious Person, (for I own it is with some Difficulty I can believe it to be the first Performance of a young Poet;) whoever he be, I say, he must be allow'd to have the genuine Spirit of sublime Poetry in him, and bids fair to reach at length the Heighth of *Milton's* Character; beyond which I think he need not aspire."[44] A second edition of *Winter* was printed in June, with a preface by Thomson extolling the "grand works of Nature" as the fittest subject for poetry. He was now well launched into a venture which carried him through *Summer, Spring, Autumn,* and "A Hymn on the Seasons" by 1730.

Thomson's first literary connections in London were with the circle of Aaron Hill, a journalist, dramatist, and poet well known in his own day but forgotten in ours. Included in this circle were Mallet, John Dyer, Richard Savage, and others. Hill encouraged flattery; and Thomson responded in the expected manner to Hill's praises of *Winter,* overanxious undoubtedly to secure for himself an important connection:

> I will not affect a moderate Joy at your Approbation, your Praise: It pleases, it delights, it ravishes me! Forgive me for the Lowness of the Truth, when I vow, I'd rather have it than the Acclamations of Thousands: 'Tis so sincere, so delicate, so distinguishing, so glowing, and, what peculiarly marks and endears it, so beautifully generous.
>
> That great Mind, and transcendent Humanity, that appear in the Testimony you have been pleas'd to give my first Attempt, would have utterly confounded me, if I had not been prepar'd for such an Entertainment, by your well-known Character; which the Voice of Fame, and your own masterly Writings, loudly proclaim.[45]

An unfortunate aspect of Thomson's entire career is that he never established himself quite well enough to throw off the yoke of subserviency which demanded flattering dedications and time-serving tasks for Hill, Dodington, Lyttelton, Prince Frederick, and others who patronized him at one time or another. But this was a disease of the time, and Thomson actually withstood it better than many others. The indifference of the early Hanoverian kings to literature and the refusal by Robert Walpole to patronize honest writers set a bad example for both noblemen and politicians who had patronized authors in the past. On the other hand, the heyday of the booksellers, who later in the century sold books to an increasingly prosperous and literate middle class and thus made it possible for a competent author to live by his own resources, was barely dawning in Thomson's day. Therefore, as the number of patrons dwindled, the flattery grew more fulsome. In 1753, the novelist Tobias Smollett, Thomson's friend and fellow Scot, reported that Thomson had smarted severely under the system: "[Thomson] was so often put to the blush for the undeserved incense he had offered in the heat of an enthusiastic disposition, misled by popular applause, that he had resolved to retract, in his last will, all the encomiums which he had thus prematurely bestowed, and stigmatise the unworthy by name—a laudable scheme of poetical justice, the execution of which was fatally prevented by untimely death."[46]

In May, 1726, Thomson obtained a position as "Tutor to a Young Gentleman" at Watt's Academy in Little Tower-street in London. This Academy was at the time the center of a vigorous popularization of Newton's philosophy; and Thomson's interest in Newton and Newtonianism, which he probably had developed first in Edinburgh, must have been increased substantially during his stay at the Academy. During the summer and autumn of 1726 he was writing *Summer*. Mallet was at the same time working on his poem *The Excursion*, and the two poets exchanged criticisms of each other's work. In a piece of advice Thomson gave Mallet about *The Excursion*, we find a prescription which he was certainly applying also to his own efforts in writing *The Seasons:* "My Idea of your Poem is a Description of the grand Works of Nature, raised, and animated by moral, and sublime, Reflections. . . . Sublimity must be the Characteristic of your Piece."[47] For Thomson's descriptions are always followed by "suitable Reflections"; and nature is the fittest subject for poetry because it provides more which "enlarges and transports the soul" than other subjects.

Summer was published by Millan in February, 1727, and dedicated to George Bubb Dodington, who became Thomson's chief patron until about 1735. Dodington was a member of Walpole's government, a time-serving politician who "raised toadyism to almost sublime proportions"[48] and who later kept a diary which is today considered "a monument to the corruption of his age" and "one of the cardinal documents of eighteenth-century politics."[49] The connection with Dodington may well be one of those which Thomson told Smollett he meant to renounce in his will; but from 1727 to 1735 he and Dodington were very close. Thomson addressed Dodington as "the British Maecenas," in whom "the Virtues, the Graces, and the Muses join their influence" (1727); as "the happy man, [in whose mind] judgement sits clear-sighted, and surveys/The chain of reason with unerring gaze" (1729); and as one by whom he was "fired with the restless thirst/Of thy applause" (1730).[50] Dodington subscribed to twenty copies of *The Seasons* in 1730, served as Thomson's principal correspondent in England when the poet was abroad from 1730 to 1733, and frequently entertained him at his home at Eastbury in Dorsetshire. Dodington was probably Thomson's first link with Frederick, prince of Wales, whose interests Thomson later served for several years. Dodington seems to have been the chief adviser to the prince in the early 1730s; and the fact that Thomson passed from Dodington's hands into George Lyttelton's, the prince's new favorite, in the mid-1730s when Dodington fell into disfavor, is one notable example of the unfortunate necessity he felt to attach himself to influential patrons.

Thomson's next publication was *A Poem Sacred to the Memory of Sir Isaac Newton,* brought out by Millan on May 8, 1727. This is one of Thomson's important poems, closely related to *The Seasons,* and will be discussed in chapter 2. Thomson dedicated the poem flatteringly to that "most illustrious *Patriot,*" Sir Robert Walpole, a fact interesting in view of his slighting references to Walpole's policies in *Britannia* only two years later and his full-fledged attacks on the government in the late 1730s when he was writing for the prince's party. Actually, Thomson was simply casting about in these early years for patronage wherever a possibility glimmered; and his patron Dodington, a member of the government, may have advised him to try Walpole. Thomson had dedicated *Winter* in 1726 to Sir Spencer Compton, then speaker of the House of Commons and thought to be a likely candidate to succeed Walpole as prime minister on the death of George I. Thomson had thus canvassed both possibilities for patronage by the prime minister. Walpole was notorious for his neglect of writers (except hireling journalists); and Thomson gained nothing substantial from his flattery of either Compton or Walpole. Thus it is not surprising that he, like many another writer of the time, began to drift toward the Opposition.

In January of 1728 Thomson wrote to Sir John Clerk that "I am now almost done with the four Seasons; and by the Advice and Encouragement of several Friends have published Proposals for printing them by Subscription."[51] These proposals soon appeared in several London newspapers. Thomson apparently did not at first intend to issue *Spring* as a separate publication; but subscriptions at one guinea for the proposed quarto volume came in discouragingly slow, and *Spring* was published in June, 1728. Subscriptions continued to lag; and the collected edition, with *Autumn* and "A Hymn on the Seasons" added, was not published for two more years. *Spring* was brought out not by Millan but by Andrew Millar, another young Scottish bookseller who remained Thomson's publisher and close friend throughout the poet's life. Their arrangement was mutually agreeable: Thomson's writings provided one of the main staples of Millar's business for many years, and he was in turn generous with Thomson. According to Murdoch, "Mr. *Millar* was always at hand, to answer, or even to prevent, his demands."[52] Millar's proprietary interest in Thomson continued long after the poet's death. He allotted the profits from a handsome two-volume quarto edition of Thomson's works in 1762 to erect a monument to the poet in Westminster Abbey; and at the time of his death in 1768 was engaged in a classic copyright lawsuit over the infringement of his rights to *The Seasons.* An honest, generous, and increasingly successful bookseller like Millar provided the only chance for writers like Thomson to escape the declining and degrading patronage system; but most of them, including Thomson, never made quite enough money to be able to forsake the search for the pensions, sinecures, and other forms of support that a patron could provide.

Murdoch says, "From that time [publication of *Winter* in 1726] Mr. *Thomson's* acquaintance was courted by all men of taste; and several ladies of high rank and distinction became his declared patronesses: the Countess of *Hertford,* Miss *Drelincourt,* afterwards Viscountess *Primrose,* Mrs. *Stanley,* and others."[53] Of these noble ladies, the countess of Hertford figures most prominently in Thomson's career. Her friend Mrs. Elizabeth Rowe called her attention to Thomson's *Winter* soon after its publication in 1726; and the countess invited the poet during the summer of 1727 to visit her at Marlborough Castle, where he wrote at least a part of *Spring.* When he published *Spring* in June, 1728, Thomson dedicated the poem to the countess, with the usual flattering remarks about her "mind exalted," "heart overflowing with humanity," and "the whole train of virtues thence derived." Dr. Johnson's story that Thomson forfeited any later invitations to visit the countess by his insensitivity to her own poetic endeavors was thoroughly discredited in 1928 by Helen Sard Hughes, who examined papers of the Percy family at Alnwick Castle which show "abundant evidence of the continued interest of the Countess in Thomson, and of some measure of friendly intercourse between them from 1727 until Thomson's death in 1748."[54] Since 1723 the countess had been lady of the bedchamber to Princess Caroline (queen after June, 1727); and she was instrumental in gaining for Thomson Queen Caroline's support for his subscription *Seasons* and for *Sophonisba,* his first play. But the queen's patronage was short-lived, due to Thomson's increasing involvement in the 1730s with the Opposition party.

The countess also figures in Thomson's life as one of the first of a succession of ladies with whom he fell deeply in love and who even influenced his writing to some extent. The best known of these women is of course Elizabeth Young, who later figures in *The Seasons* and other poems as "Amanda." Thomson, although he never married, had a fond and foolish heart where women were concerned. To this his letters are ample testimony. "To turn my Eyes a softer Way, I am really touched with a fair Neighbour of your's—You know Who—Absence sighs it to me. What is my Heart made of? A soft System or Love—Nerves—Too sensible for my Quiet," he wrote to David Mallet in 1729.[55] The friendly, attractive countess, nearly his own age, apparently affected him strongly. He gave her, probably during his visit to Marlborough Castle in 1727, the following "song":

Hard is the Fate of Him who loves,
  Yet dares not tell his trembling Pain,
But to the sympathetic Groves,
  But to the lonely listning Plain.

Oh when She blesses next your Shade,
  Oh when her Foot-steps next are seen,
In flowery Tracts along the Mead,
  In fresher Mazes o'er the Green;

Some gentle Spirit of the Vale,
  To whom the weeping Lover's dear,
From dying Lillies waft a Gale,
  And sigh my Sorrows in her Ear.

Oh tell Her what She cannot blame,
  Tho Fear my Tongue must ever bind,
Oh tell Her that my heavenly Flame
  Is as her sacred Soul refin'd.

Not her own guardian Angel eyes
  With chaster Extasy his Care,
Not purer her own Wishes rise,
  Not holier her own Sighs in Prayer.

Let Heaven and Her but this bestow,
  (Can aught that's tender this deny?)
Oft! oft! to hear her Goodness flow,
  And drink the Vertues from her Eye:

For Angels warble when She speaks;
  And where her Eyes, sweet-beaming, shine
Heaven on th'extatic Gazer breaks,
  Inspiring Something all-divine.[56]

Also, Thomson was given to introducing his own sentimental feelings into *The Seasons,* although by techniques which serve to conceal somewhat their subjectivity;[57] and it is likely that the long "tortured lover" passage in *Spring* (ll. 1004–73) can be linked autobiographically to Thomson's "trembling Pain" for the countess, particularly since there are substantial similarities in situation and phrasing between the poem given to the countess and the passage in *Spring.* Like the sorrowful lover in the passage quoted above, the "melancholy" lover of *Spring* seeks out "sympathetic glooms," where a "wafted spirit flies / To the vain bosom of his distant fair," while he lies "amid drooping lilies, [and] swells the breeze / With sighs unceasing, and the brook with tears" (ll. 1020–21, 1031–32).

While continuing to drum up subscriptions for *The Seasons* in 1728 and 1729, Thomson wrote *Britannia;* four short poems for inclusion in James Ralph's miscellany volume of 1729; and *Sophonisba,* his first play. *Britannia,* published anonymously January 21, 1729, was the opening move of Thomson's long involvement with patriotic themes in his poetry and drama. As a significant prelude to *Liberty* and "Rule, Britannia," *Britannia* will be discussed more fully in chapter 3. This poem was Thomson's contribution to the increasing popular demand for war with Spain during 1727–1729. Fear of Spanish claims to Gibraltar and indignation over her manhandling of

English merchantmen in the West Indies combined to stir increasing resentment over Walpole's peace policy. The pages of the chief Opposition journal, the *Craftsman,* show agitation over the Spanish question to have been at fever pitch from November, 1728, to mid-1729.[58] Thomson timed his own appeal for action to coincide exactly with the opening of Parliament on January 21, 1729. *Britannia* was also timely in its compliment to Prince Frederick, that "ROYAL YOUTH" and promise of "future Glory," who had landed at Harwich on December 3, 1728. Thomson's reflections on Walpole's peace policy and his compliments to Frederick, whose position as rallying point for the Opposition was to develop later, cannot be interpreted as adverse to the king and queen, whose support he solicited and enjoyed as late as 1730. *Britannia* is a hedging performance, chiding the government on the one hand: "Whence this unwonted Patience? this weak Doubt?" but on the other hand praising peace and "the Man divine, who gives us Thee,"[59] which could easily have been interpreted as a reference to Walpole. But *Britannia* shows clearly the drift toward Thomson's later active participation in the Opposition.

In April, 1729, four of Thomson's poems were published in James Ralph's *Miscellaneous Poems by Several Hands.* He had enough stature and reputation by this time to be among those listed "Particularly" on the title page, along with Swift, Garth, John Hughes, and the duke of Wharton. These four poems, all in couplets, show Thomson continuing to experiment with a variety of forms and themes. "A Paraphrase on the Latter Part of the VIth Chapter of St. Matthew" is undistinguished. "The Incomparable Soporific Doctor" is a satire on a dull, well-fed priest in the vein of Pope's *Dunciad.* The identification of the "Doctor" with Thomson's friend Patrick Murdoch, made by several of Thomson's biographers and editors, is almost certainly erroneous. Murdoch was too good a friend to be attacked so viciously and besides was not "Parsonifyed" until 1738. Thomson's basically benign, sentimental, and "enthusiast" temperament did not lead him to develop further this uncharacteristic attempt at witty, humorous satirical attack. "The Happy Man" fails to transcend its immediate function as a compliment to Dodington; but it does foreshadow Thomson's considerable interest in the ideal man of virtue, benevolence, or patriotism. "Hymn on Solitude," a Miltonic lyric which imitates "Il Penseroso" in tone, measure, and structure, is an important poem and will be discussed in chapter 4.

Thomson saw the first of his five classical tragedies, *Sophonisba,* acted at Drury Lane on February 28, 1730. He had been thinking of writing a play for at least two years; and it was natural that, as a member of Aaron Hill's circle, he should do so. Hill was keenly interested in the stage and was at one time or another theater manager, playwright, author of a theatrical periodical, and highly successful adapter of Voltaire's tragedies for the English stage. Attempts at tragedy were characteristic of writers patronized by Hill. Thomson's fellow Scotsmen Joseph Mitchell and David Mallet were aided by Hill in staging tragedies. Richard Savage had written and produced *Sir Thomas Overbury* under Hill's patronage in 1723. Edward Young, who had connections with Hill's group and was one of Thomson's earliest acquaintances in London, had staged two tragedies, *Busiris* (1719) and *The Revenge* (1721). Besides, drama was by far the most profitable form of literary activity at the time; and a poet of slender means but with ambitions to succeed as a writer in London found the theatrical prospect hugely attractive. Thomson's venture into the writing of tragedy can also be seen as an attempt to progress from descriptive poetry to a nobler, higher form of art. In an age which adhered to a recognized hierarchy of literary forms of which epic and tragedy were the highest, Thomson aspired to higher rungs of the ladder. That he saw himself in such terms is borne out by his statement to Dodington in late 1730 that "My heart both trembles with diffidence and burns with ardor" at the thought of writing an epic.[60] Early admirers of *The Seasons* expected that Thomson would go on to "higher" forms. A critic of *The Seasons* expressed in 1728 his approval of Thomson's plan to write a tragedy: "May I have leave just to hint that the *present* Encouragement of so good a Genius may prove *their future* Entertainment in a nobler way; when the Author shall rise from the *still Life* of Poetry, to represent the Passions of Mankind, those great Springs of Action; and the Distresses flowing from them, which, by exciting our Compassion and Fear, move and delight so exquisitely in the *Scene*."[61] Thomson's ambitions would also have been aroused by the critic who had written in 1726 that he "bids fair to reach at length the Heighth of *Milton's* Character."[62] By the end of 1730, he had succeeded with a long descriptive poem and had seen his tragedy *Sophonisba* acted to applause for ten nights on the London stage. His chief models, Virgil and Milton, had both crowned their careers with epic performances. It was thus natural that Thomson should at this time turn his thoughts to the possibility that he might indeed make his own name immortal by writing eventually a great patriotic epic.

In June, 1730, the subscription quarto of *The Seasons,* with *Autumn* and "A Hymn on the Seasons" added for the first time, made its appearance. "A Poem Sacred to the Memory of Sir Isaac Newton" was also included. The book was printed on "superfine Royal Paper" with five plates by William Kent; and it remains today an impressive book, beautifully designed and printed. The list of subscribers, headed by Queen Caroline, includes 387 names, several of them down for multiple copies. The Scotch nobility subscribed heavily; but many Englishmen also contributed, including several prominent noblemen and men of letters. Alexander Pope showed his particular desire to support Thomson by subscribing for three books. A copy, now in the Yale Library, is inscribed in Pope's hand as a gift from Thomson. Other surviving evidence shows a close and friendly association between Pope and Thomson, a fact generally ignored by the school of criticism which has represented them as diametrically opposed neoclassicist and preromantic, trying to "beat down" one another.

In November, 1730, Thomson opened a new phase of his career by embarking on his own version of the grand tour of Europe. On October 27, he wrote to Valentine Munbee, "I travell along with Mr Talbot the Sollicitor's son, and we propose to set out for Paris in about ten days hence."[63] According to Murdoch, Dr. Thomas Rundle, a prominent clergyman who had taken an interest in Thomson's work, first recommended him to the influential Talbot family,[64] a connection from which Thomson was to reap great benefit. He was now employed as traveling companion to Charles Richard Talbot, son of Charles Talbot, then solicitor-general and later, from 1733 to his death in 1737, the lord chancellor. Thomson wrote enthusiastically of his new prospects to Dodington: "Travelling has been long my fondest wish for the very purpose you recommend: the storing one's Imagination with Ideas of all-beautiful, all-great, and all-perfect Nature. These are the true materia poetica, the light and colours with which Fancy kindles up her whole creation, paints a sentiment, and even embodies an abstracted thought. I long to see the feilds whence Virgil gathered his immortal honey, and to tread the same ground where men have thought and acted so greatly!"[65] Exact information about Thomson's tour is scarce. He wrote to Dodington from Paris on December 27, 1730, and from Rome on November 28, 1731. A letter to the countess of Hertford from Paris on October 10, 1732, must have been written shortly before his return to England in late 1732 or 1733; but the specific date of his return is unknown.

From a literary standpoint, the significance of this tour is that it provided Thomson fuel for his long blank-verse poem *Liberty* (1735–36), a patriotic and enthusiastic exposition of Whig doctrine, which was simmering in his mind as he pondered scenes of classical greatness now ruined by "bad Government . . . and perticularly that of the Priests, [which] has not only extirpated almost human Arts and Industry, but even disfigured Nature herself."[66] An exalted conception of patriotic love and service to one's own country is one of the most significant elements in Thomson's work considered as a whole; and he went abroad, like other properly indoctrinated young Englishmen of the time, with definite preconceptions of what he would find. Almost as soon as he set foot on French soil, he wrote to Dodington:

> I have seen little of Paris yet [—] some streets and playhouses; though, had I seen all that is to be seen here, you know it too well to need a much better account than I can give. You must, however, give me leave to observe, that amidst all that external and shewy magnificence which the French affect, one misses that solid magnificence of trade and sincere plenty which not only appears to be, but is, substantially, in a kingdom where industry and liberty mutually support and inspirit each other. That kingdom, I suppose, I need not mention, as it is, and ever will be, sufficiently plain from the character. I shall return no worse Englishman than I came away.[67]

By November, 1731, he was writing to Dodington, "That Enthusiasm I had upon me with regard to travelling goes off, I find, very fast. One may imagine fine things in reading of antient authors, but to travel is to dissipate that vision."[68] As he traveled, Thomson "moved from the vague enthusiasm of the young traveler to an increasingly severe moral and political didacticism."[69] By October, 1732, he was expressing to the countess of Hertford indignant and exalted political sentiments on the state of modern Italy which show that part 1 of *Liberty* was already in his mind. Thomson had moved in two years from a vague plan for "a *poetical* landscape of countries, mixed with moral observations on their governments and people,"[70] similar perhaps to the plan of *The Seasons,* to the primarily political viewpoint which characterizes *Liberty.*

Thomson was back in London at least by early 1733. While abroad, he had written an elegy for the painter William Aikman, one of his earliest friends in London, who had died in June, 1731. Thomson told the countess of Hertford that these verses "are rather a plain testimony of Friendship, than an attempt of poetry."[71] Perhaps it is because he was not attempting to be "poetical" that the closing lines achieve a sincerity and simplicity rarely to be found in his poetry:

> As those we love decay, we die in part,
> String after string is severed from the heart;
> Till loosened life, at last but breathing clay,
> Without one pang is glad to fall away.
> Unhappy he who latest feels the blow,
> Whose eyes have wept o'er every friend laid low,
> Dragged lingering on from partial death to death,
> Till, dying, all he can resign is breath.[72]

III *Patriotism and Politics, 1733–1740*

Thomson apparently spent the period 1733–1735 almost entirely at work on *Liberty,* a work for which he had great hopes and undoubtedly considered a higher and nobler effort than anything earlier attempted. He experienced a sad blow when his young traveling companion, Charles Richard Talbot, died in September, 1733. But his fortunes "blossomed pretty well" under the patronage of the elder Talbot, newly made lord chancellor, who gave him, probably in 1734, the lucrative sinecure of secretary of the briefs. Thomson was "far advanced" in the writing of *Liberty* by November, 1733;[73] and he was near enough to completion by December, 1734, to sell the copyright to Millar for 250 pounds. Part 1, *Antient and Modern Italy Compared,* was published January 13, 1735; part 2, *Greece,* was published on February 7; and part 3, *Rome,* was published on March 24. Part 4, *Britain,* was published about nine months later in mid-January, 1736; and part 5, *The Prospect,* followed in mid-February. The failure of *Liberty* to attract readers from the very beginning is dismally documented in the ledger of the printer Henry Woodfall.[74] Millar, who had paid dearly for the copyright and obviously expected a large sale, ambitiously ordered 3,250 copies of part 1. Sales must have lagged from the beginning, for orders for parts 2 and 3 were immediately cut by 1,000 copies each. When parts 4 and 5 were published nearly a year later, only 1,250 copies of each were printed. Thomson told Aaron Hill on May 11, 1736, that he was thinking about annulling the copyright sale to Millar, "who would else be a considerable Loser, by the Paper, Printing, and Publication, of Liberty."[75]

The failure of *Liberty* is of great significance in understanding Thomson's career as a writer. He had succeeded with *The Seasons* and, at least for his contemporaries, with tragedy. He then aspired to move on to something "nobler" and as early as 1730 was thinking of an epic, an understandable ambition for one whose models were Virgil, Milton, and Spenser and who had been encouraged by his contemporaries to think of himself as a poet of great potential. *Liberty* is not of course an epic; but it could be called "epic-like," certainly "heroic" in the vast scope and exalted manner in which its historical and political themes are treated. Thus *Liberty* fits into an accepted scheme of a poet's development which could be called "classical" and which in theory would have led Thomson from early pastorals and imitations through *The Seasons* (patterned on Virgil's *Georgics*), classical tragedy, *Liberty,* and finally to the epic which would hopefully make his name immortal. In doing so, he would be following in the footsteps of Virgil, Milton, and Spenser. Speaking of *Liberty,* Murdoch says, ". . . he employed two years of his life in composing that noble work: upon which, conscious of the importance and dignity of the subject, he valued himself more than upon all his other writings."[76] The failure of *Liberty* was one of the greatest discouragements of Thomson's life. A natural indolence is sometimes said to be responsible for his relative lack of activity in later life, but with the failure of *Liberty* a pattern had been broken which could not be reestablished. He first hoped to revise *Liberty,* but after revising part 1 and making a few changes in part 2 he dropped the project. He then occupied his pen during the period 1737–1740 in the service of his patrons Lyttelton and Prince Frederick and the frenzied opposition to Walpole. In the early 1740s he lapsed into a period of inactivity and dissipation which caused concern among his friends. In 1743–44, hoping to make enough money to marry Elizabeth Young, he roused himself to an extensive revision of *The Seasons* and the writing of another play. In his last years, he returned to some Spenserian stanzas which he had written years earlier "in the way of raillery on himself, and on some of his friends, who would reproach him with indolence,"[77] and expanded them into a minor masterpiece, *The Castle of Indolence* (1748). But given his earlier ambitions, it is hardly likely that Thomson himself thought of this poem as a suitable climax to his career. There is something poignantly autobiographical about these lines from *The Castle of Indolence,* published shortly before his death:

But how shall I attempt such arduous String?
I who have spent my Nights, and nightly Days,
In this Soul-deadening Place, loose-loitering?
Ah! how shall I for this uprear my moulted Wing?

Come on, my Muse, nor stoop to low Despair,
Thou imp of *Jove,* touch'd by celestial Fire!
Thou yet shalt sing of War, and Actions fair,
Which the bold sons of BRITAIN will inspire;
Of antient Bards thou yet shalt sweep the Lyre;
Thou yet shalt tread in Tragic Pall the Stage,
Paint Love's enchanting Woes, the Heroe's Ire,
The Sage's Calm, the Patriot's noble Rage,
Dashing Corruption down through every worthless Age.[78]

Thus Thomson's great posthumous reputation, based almost entirely on *The Seasons* and *The Castle of Indolence,* represents a paradox. For he continued to the end of his days to believe that heroic efforts—tragedy and epic—were the poet's hope of future fame and glory. Perhaps they are, in the long run. But Thomson was not Virgil or Milton; and the age in which he lived, despite its aspirations, did not produce lasting epic or tragedy.

Some measure of Thomson's stature in London by the mid-1730s is provided by a note in the *Gentleman's Magazine* for June, 1736. Here it is announced that 102 "Noblemen and Gentlemen" have formed a Society for the Encouragement of Learning. James Thomson was one of twenty-four named to a "Committee of Managers" for the organization. In mid-1736 Thomson also established a permanent home in Kew-Lane, Richmond, not far from Alexander Pope's house at Twickenham. Douglas Grant has pointed out that Thomson occupied two houses in Kew-Lane, moving to the larger of the two in 1739.[79] A catalog prepared for the sale of Thomson's effects after his death shows his house to have been furnished comfortably and with a degree of elegance. Thomson and his neighbor Pope, who had long been acquainted, seem to have lived on terms of friendliness and even intimacy. Pope, as a partisan of Prince Frederick, spent much time helping Thomson, David Mallet, and Aaron Hill stage their political tragedies in the late 1730s; but he and Thomson were fond of each other's company on other than political terms. William Robertson, a close friend of Thomson, later recalled that Pope visited Thomson frequently: "Pope has sometimes said, Thomson, I'll walk to the end of your garden, and then set off to the bottom of Kew-foot-lane and back. Pope, sir, courted Thomson, and Thomson was always admitted to Pope whether he had company or not."[80] William Taylor, Thomson's barber at Richmond, when asked in later years whether Pope often visited Thomson, replied: "Very often; he used to wear a light-coloured great coat, and commonly kept it on in the house; he was a strange, ill-formed, little figure of a man; but I have heard him and Quin, and Paterson, talk together so at Thomson's, that I could have listened to them for ever."[81]

The years 1737–1740 mark the period of Thomson's most active political involvement. The political background of the 1730s is extremely complicated; but the important thing to note here is that Thomson came near to entirely sacrificing his muse at this time to political considerations, and a few general remarks on the political background must suffice. Robert Walpole, the "prime minister" from 1721 to 1742, was for various reasons faced after 1726 with a vigorous "Opposition" which reached a crescendo from 1736 to 1742, when he was finally toppled by his foes. Partly because of the indifference of Walpole and George II to deserving authors, many of them were inclined to support the Opposition. A frontal assault on Walpole's government was carried on throughout the period in the *Craftsman,* the bitingly satirical and well-managed Opposition newspaper. A leading light of the *Craftsman* and for a time center of the Opposition was Lord Bolingbroke, the brilliant Tory from Queen Anne's ministry who had fled to France at the Hanoverian accession but who had been allowed to return, albeit under crippling political restrictions, in 1725. Frederick, prince of Wales after 1727, was disliked by his parents King George and Queen Caroline, who reluctantly gave in to public opinion and allowed the prince to come to England in 1728. Frederick's relations with his parents grew gradually worse; and by 1737, during which year he was angrily banished entirely from his father's court, he had become the willing rallying point of the Opposition party, whose feud with Walpole was increasingly marked on both sides by overt hatred and vindictiveness. George Lyttelton and William Pitt, the future earl of Chatham, had by antiadministration speeches in Parliament in 1736 made themselves the leaders of a band of "boy-patriots," a group of intelligent young men despised with particular bitterness by both Walpole and George II. After Prince Frederick's open breach with his father in September, 1737, he immediately set up what amounted to an Opposition court. In October, 1737, he made Lyttelton his secretary and appointed Pitt a groom of the bedchamber. Lyttelton's particular forte was the recruiting of authors for active service in the prince's cause, and Thomson was one of his first recruits.

Thomson's open support of the Opposition beginning in 1737 represents rather a shift in strategy than a complete change of position. As early as 1729 he had criticized the government and complimented Prince Frederick in *Britannia.* Even while abroad in the early 1730s, he had continued to seek the prince's favor, perhaps at the urging of his patron Dodington, who up to about 1734 was Frederick's chief adviser and favorite. *Liberty,* which has been called an "Opposition poem," was dedicated in enthusiastic terms to Prince Frederick. *Liberty* does echo many of the *Craftsman*'s disaffected ideas of the state of England, but mostly in general statements which do not pointedly attack the government. The dedication to Frederick cannot be taken to mean that Thomson identified himself openly with the Opposition while writing *Liberty.* The poem was pretty well completed by the end of 1734; and it is a mistake to believe that Frederick, in spite of the conflict with his parents, was much involved with the Opposition party before about 1736. Frederick is not mentioned prominently or praised in the *Craftsman,* for example, until late 1735. The displacement of Dodington by Lyttelton as the prince's chief adviser in the mid-1730s was a result of Dodington's policy of encouraging conciliation between Frederick and the court. Lord Hervey, who gives us our most intimate picture of the backstairs politics of this period, says: "Mr. Lyttelton, a nephew of Lord Cobham's, whom Dodington had brought about the Prince, had contributed too to this [Dodington's] disgrace; for Dodington, from irresolution, or fear of throwing the Prince . . . into the hand of those who were at the head of the opposing party, had dissuaded the Prince from going those lengths to which Lord Cobham and Lord Chesterfield, who were exasperated to the last degree against the Court, wished to drive him."[82] After 1736 or 1737, continued support of the prince almost inevitably demanded a corresponding attack on the government; and Thomson took the step. Dodington, who had been his chief patron for most of his writing career, simply vanished from his life after 1735. His new patron and "great friend" was George Lyttelton, who somewhat officiously controlled his fortunes for the remainder of Thomson's life and even felt himself qualified to "correct and emend" extensively in the posthumous publication of the poet's works. Another factor in Thomson's shift of strategy in 1737 may have been the death of Lord Chancellor Talbot on February 14 of that year and the resulting loss by Thomson of his lucrative government sinecure. He published in June a flattering elegy, "To the Memory of the Right Honourable the Lord Talbot." In the autumn of 1737 Thomson, on the recommendation of Lyttelton, received a pension of 100 pounds a year from Prince Frederick.

Thomson's first contribution after joining the campaign was a poem, "To His Royal Highness the Prince of Wales: An Ode on the Birth of the Princess Augusta," published in several magazines and newspapers during September and October, 1737. Princess Augusta's birth on August 1 had been the occasion of a gross insult by Frederick to his parents. In defiance of a royal decree that the child should be born at Hampton Court, he secretly and somewhat brutally moved his wife during her labor to St. James's Palace, where the child was born. This defiant act proved the last straw in the increasingly bitter relations between the prince and his parents; and in early September the king ordered the prince to leave St. James as soon as his wife was able to travel and further decreed that "no Person whatsoever, who shall go to pay their Court to their Royal Highnesses the Prince and Princess of Wales, shall be admitted into his Majesty's Presence at any of the Royal Palaces."[83] The publication of Thomson's "Ode" was timed to correspond almost exactly with the departure of Frederick from St. James in mid-September; and its tone was defiant:

I

While *secret-leaguing* Nations frown around,
  Ready to pour the long-expected Storm;
While SHE, who wont the restless *Gaul* to bound,
  BRITANNIA, drooping, grows an empty Form;
While on our Vitals *selfish-Parties* prey,
And deep *Corruption* eats our Soul away:
. . . .

V

May fate my fond devoted Days extend,
  To sing the promis'd Glories of THY REIGN!
What tho', by Years depres'd, my *Muse* might bend;
  My Heart will teach her still a nobler Strain:
How, with *recover'd* BRITAIN, will she soar!
When *Fr——e* INSULTS, and *Sp——n* shall Rob no more![84]

Thomson continued to use his pen in the service of the Opposition by writing a preface for Millar's publication of Milton's *Areopagitica* in January, 1738. The political timeliness of this can best be understood by reference to the Walpole-sponsored stage licensing act of June 21, 1737. The Opposition immediately raised a hue and cry that the liberty of the press was being threatened. Lord Chesterfield said in a famous speech before Parliament that "It is an Arrow that does but glance upon the Stage; but it will give a fatal wound to the Liberty of the Press."[85] The Opposition papers *Craftsman* and *Common Sense* loudly repeated the same theme; and a particularly outspoken paper in the *Craftsman* on July 2 brought swift and severe government retribution. The hapless printer was tried and sentenced, his shop closed and his accounts seized, and publication stopped for a time. Walpole's official organ, the *Daily Gazetteer,* denounced the July 2 *Craftsman* paper as "the greatest Insult, and most notorious Abuse, that was ever offered to the supreme Power or chief Magistrate of any Country, in any Age or Nation."[86]

In March, 1738, the Opposition again appropriated a work by Milton for political purposes when Millar published *A Manifesto of the Lord Protector of the Commonwealth of England, Scotland, Ireland, Etc.,* "Wherein is shewn the Reasonableness of the cause of this Republic against the Depredations of the Spaniards." Grievances against Spain—and Walpole's reluctance to do anything about them—had been one of the *Craftsman*'s main targets in the late 1720s; by the late 1730s, these grievances had been compounded and aggravated until the "depredations of the Spaniards" had become the popular outcry, an outcry encouraged, of course, by the Opposition. In 1739, Walpole was to be forced into war with Spain, "amidst the rejoicings of the mob, the ringing of bells, and the prince of Wales toasting the multitude from a city tavern."[87] The following lines from Thomson's *Britannia* were used as an epigraph in the republication of Milton's 1655 *Manifesto:*

> Whence is it that the proud *Iberian* thus,
> In their own well-asserted Element,
> Dares rouze to Wrath the Masters of the Main?
> Who told him, that the big incumbent War
> Would not, ere this, have roll'd his trembling Ports
> In smoky Ruin?[88]

Britannia was included in its entirety at the end of the *Manifesto.*

Thomson's return to the London stage after eight years was sponsored by the Opposition, now the "prince's party." *Agamemnon,* staged at Drury Lane on April 6, 1738, succeeded on the stage and sold extremely well in printed form primarily because of a thinly disguised, vicious attack on Walpole. *Edward and Eleonora,* intended to compliment Prince Frederick at the expense of his father and Walpole, was to have been staged at Covent Garden on March 29, 1739, but was "forbid to be acted" by Walpole's licenser, now more on the alert after the obviously political success of *Agamemnon.* Thomson's tragedies and their political contexts will be more fully discussed in chapter 3. The climax of Thomson's service in the prince's cause was *Alfred: A Masque,* written in collaboration with David Mallet and performed privately at Cliveden before the prince and princess of Wales on August 1, 1740. The performance was climaxed by the singing of "Rule Britannia" in the last scene. If Thomson had been led to use his pen for narrow and perhaps somewhat ignoble political purposes, his essential patriotism here reasserted itself and transcended the politics of 1740 to produce a great national ode, "patriotic" in a larger sense: "Rule, *Britannia,* rule the waves;/ *Britons* never will be slaves."

Thomson continued until his death in 1748 to enjoy the patronage of Lyttelton, and he even kept his pension from the prince for several years and was given another government sinecure after Lyttelton assumed a government position in 1744; but he was never again called upon to exercise his pen in the service of a frenzied "Opposition," which lost its target when Walpole was forced into war in 1739, gradually lost ground, and was forced to resign in February, 1742.

IV *Later Life, 1741–1748*

James Thomson did not survive his middle age. Even if he had, it is unlikely that later work would have added much to his reputation. *The Castle of Indolence,* published in the year of his death, is his most polished and skillful poem; but it was written in spite of—and in some ways as by-product of—an increasingly comfortable and sluggish existence which contrasts sharply with the early vigor, enthusiasm, and ambition with which he had written *The Seasons, Sophonisba,* and *Liberty.* It is hard to escape the conclusion that Thomson's later years were spent more in the company of amiable friends, his couch, and his bottle than in seeking the Muse. The failure of *Liberty;* the funneling of his energies into politics for several intense years; a bitterly disappointing love affair in the early 1740s: all these took their toll and broke the pattern which both he and his contemporaries had earlier seen developing in his career. In the early 1740s Thomson was receiving hints from his friends "with Regard to Regularity and Temperance."[89] On September 7, 1742, Lady Hertford wrote to one of her friends: "I have not seen Thomson almost these three Years he keeps Company with scarce any Body but Mallet & one or two of the Players, & indeed hardly any body else will keep Company with him, He turns Day into Night, & Night into Day & is (as I am told) never awake till after Midnight & I doubt has quite drown'd his Genius."[90]

Beginning in late 1742, Thomson was jolted out of his lethargy by a passion of great intensity. Always susceptible to feminine charms, he now fell deeply in love with the young Scotswoman Elizabeth Young, who was a sister to the wife of his close friend William Robertson. A number of surviving letters written to Miss Young in the mid-1740s document poignantly Thomson's utter infatuation, hopelessly idealistic view of love and marriage, and increasing despair. In his first letter to her, written March 10, 1743, Thomson threw caution to the winds and declared his passion:

> What shall I say but that I love you, love you with the utmost Ardor, the most perfect Esteem, and inexpressible Tenderness. Imagination, Reason and the Heart, all conspire to love you. I may venture to say, without Extravagance, I love you better than my own Soul. My Happiness is only a secondary Consideration to yours, can alone consist in making you happy: there is no Happiness for me but in passing my Life with you, in devoting it to please you. Never had one Being a stronger Propensity to seek the Good of another than I to seek yours: to gain that dearest Purpose all Fortune if in my Power would seem Dross, Toil Ease, and Pain Pleasure. I shall be thought romantic, and yet the most passionate Expressions upon this Occasion are poor to what I feel. My Heart labours, is oppressed, with unutterable Fondness.[91]

He apparently received mild encouragement, which caused him to continue to pour out his "busy, doubting, hoping, delighted, tortured Heart" to her in frequent long letters through the summer and autumn of 1743. On September 28, although by this time the lady's caution and reserve must have given him some conviction of the slenderness of his chances, he was still writing optimistically:

> Ah my dearest Miss Young! I can have no other Idea of happy Life but with you. How miserable is it then that I should be so much absent from all that is dear and lovely to me in the World? It is impossible, I cannot support Life with out at least your Presence. How can I live at a Distance from my

Heart, especially as you will not directly assure me that I have all yours in Return? But remember I will have it, if the highest Friendship, the most exalted Love, and everlasting Tenderness can gain it. Could you refuse me your Heart, I will not have my own again, for it would then be fit for no human Purpose. Dont how ever take any Advantage over my too-much tortured Heart already, from my making this frank Declaration that I am wth unconquerable Love all yours.[92]

Although Thomson continued to write to his "dearest charming Miss Young" as late as November, 1745, that "Before next Spring I flatter myself that I shall be the happiest of Husbands,"[93] he must have given up any substantial hopes long before.

It is perhaps not an overstatement to say that this all-consuming, albeit mainly one-sided love affair provided the principal stimulus for Thomson's work during 1743-1745 and contributed something to its content and quality. In 1742 he had been halfheartedly working on the subject of Coriolanus, a project which eventually produced his feeblest drama. But he dropped this project by early 1743, when the intense infatuation with Miss Young began, to launch feverishly into the extensive and influential revision of *The Seasons,* published by Millar in July, 1744. He then set immediately to work to write his best drama, *Tancred and Sigismunda,* produced at Drury Lane on March 18, 1745. This fruitful period of activity was partly the result of Thomson's desire to prove himself to Miss Young, who chided him "with Regard to Regularity and Temperance," and more importantly, of his desire and desperate need to improve his finances to the point where he could marry. Douglas Grant is clearly accurate in remarking of Elizabeth Young, on the basis of considerably more evidence than space permits here, that "posterity owes to her influence the revised edition of *The Seasons.*"[94] The same impetus is probably responsible also for the writing of *Tancred and Sigismunda* in 1744 and 1745. That Thomson, in his last dejected letter to Elizabeth Young in November, 1745, was still promising love, friendship, and tenderness rather than any solid financial prospects is revealing and pathetic.

The Seasons has been called "not only a Nature poem but a sentimental autobiography of the poet."[95] It has already been pointed out that the "tortured lover" passage in *Spring* was probably written from the poet's own sentimental pressures. Professor Ralph Cohen, in his comprehensive study *The Unfolding of The Seasons,* comments on Thomson's "disguising" of personal sources in *The Seasons* as a major element in the poet's artistry:

> The language and thought incorporate not only external traditions but personal feelings and events. The Latinate and scientific constructions serve to create an aesthetic distance between the narrator and his private feelings. Thomson's personal involvement in the poem is concealed by these techniques at the same time that they convey his views of human experience. Thus he can talk about sex while describing flowers or about his own feelings of the pain of love by describing the ideal. These techniques are methods [to] convert and conceal his private feelings though critics have naïvely assumed that his language was 'objective' rather than an artistic instrument for disguising but not disregarding the personal sources.[96]

Clearly Elizabeth Young, to whom he gave the poetic name "Amanda," was in Thomson's mind while he was revising *The Seasons* in 1743 and early 1744. We have his own testimony that in rewriting *Spring* he was projecting a vision of his own future with Elizabeth Young in "Those Parts . . . which attempt a Picture of Virtuous happy Love."[97] That Thomson added passages to the revised *Spring* and *Summer* referring to Amanda has been frequently noted. He placed Amanda in two contexts in the revised *Spring* of 1744; and both share the unreal quality of the intensely idealized picture of Elizabeth Young worshipped in the letters of 1743. In the first passage she is a "sensuous May Virgin"[98] invited, like Herrick's Corinna, to walk among the flowers on a May morning (ll. 480–93). The image of Amanda herself is reasonably chaste, but the passage in which she appears is remarkable for the multiplicity of sexual images, with the blushing, blossoming flowers being exposed to the flying "father-dust" (l. 541), and being "loaded" by "fervent bees" tending to their "delicious task" (l. 508). The other side of the vision of happiness with Elizabeth Young in *Spring* is of course the concluding portrait of perfectly harmonious marital love and family life. This section had already been written, but Thomson revised it in 1743 and wrote to his beloved that he intended it as a vision of their own future: "O let the Picture be ours!" Autobiographical suggestion can also be seen in Thomson's complete rewriting in 1743 of the somewhat salacious story of Damon and Musidora in *Summer*. In the rewriting, Damon is made into a pining lover desperate for some assurance that his love is returned. He accidentally views Musidora disrobe for bathing, in a scene of which Ralph Cohen has remarked, "The design of the episode is to illustrate how Musidora's concealed feelings become exposed when her body is exposed."[99] When he reveals himself and flees, Musidora is moved to carve on a tree her confession of love for

Damon, a fact interesting in view of Thomson's constant imploring of Elizabeth Young to answer one of his love letters.

As in the revised *Seasons,* furthermore, *Tancred and Sigismunda* probably takes some of its coloring from the experience with Elizabeth Young. Even if Thomson was not, as Douglas Grant claims, "dramatizing his own love-affair with Elizabeth Young"[100] in the play, certainly his own personal agony at the time enabled him to write with more sympathy and understanding a pathetic tragedy of two lovers thwarted by a tyrannical parent. Thomson had also addressed several of his "Songs" to Elizabeth Young during this period, of which the following is a fairly typical example:

> Come, dear Eliza, quit the Town,
> And to the rural Hamlets fly:
> Behold, the wintry Storms are gone,
> A gentle Radiance glads the Sky.
>
> The Birds awake, the Flowers appear,
> Earth spreads a verdant Couch for thee;
> 'Tis Joy and Music all we hear,
> 'Tis Love and Beauty all we see.
>
> Come, let us mark the gradual Spring,
> How peeps the Bud, the Blossom blows;
> Till Philomel begin to sing,
> And perfect May to swell the Rose.
>
> Let us secure the short Delight,
> And wisely crop the blooming Day;
> Too soon our Spring will take it's Flight:
> Arise, my Love, and come away.[101]

If the failure of *Liberty* had dashed Thomson's exalted literary ambitions, his failure with Elizabeth Young seems to have caused him to drop likewise any ambition for the married life. When George Lyttelton proposed a match for him in 1747, he matter-of-factly replied, "I am too much advanced in Life to venture to marry, without feeling myself invigorated, and made as it were young again, with a great Flame of Imagination."[102] In the 1740s George Lyttelton assumed an increasingly large, and sometimes officious, role in Thomson's life. During the last five years of his life, Thomson visited Lyttelton frequently at Hagley Park. He was working on the revision of *The Seasons* there in the autumn of 1743, and Lyttelton intruded himself substantially into the revising process. Lyttelton, along with other members of the Opposition who had chafed and waited under Walpole, became a member of the "Broad Bottom" government in November, 1744, and immediately appointed Thomson to the lucrative sinecure of surveyor-general of the Leeward Islands. Lyttelton and William Pitt "gave instructions" at rehearsals of *Tancred and Sigismunda* in early 1745. Although *Tancred and Sigismunda* was not a political play in the sense *Agamemnon* had been, that Thomson was still being compelled to serve his masters' political purposes can be seen by the following letter of Benjamin Victor in the *Daily Post* for April 26, 1745:

> We all plainly saw by what Interest the Author of *Tancred and Sigismunda* was supported. A very remarkable new Lord of the Treasury [Lyttelton] was proud of appearing its Foster Father, and attended at the Publick Rehearsals; the first Night of the Performance this celebrated *Person,* and his Friends in the Box with him (all very lately most flaming Patriots!) were seen clapping their Hands at the following remarkable Speech:
>
> First of you All
> I here renounce those *Errors* and *Divisions;*
> That have so long disturb'd our Peace, and seem'd
> *Fermenting still* to threaten *new* Commotions;
> By *Time* instructed, let Us not disdain
> To QUIT MISTAKES.[103]

That Thomson did chafe to some extent in his new role as propagandist for the government is shown by a letter of May 31, 1745, in which he remarks: "I have undertaken again the terrible task of writing a new play [*Coriolanus*]; for, not entirely trusting to the Broad Bottom, I will try to subsist upon the narrow but sure one of Self-Independency."[104] At the very moment he was making this assertion, however, he was seeking the approval and advice of Lyttelton and Pitt for the project! As mentioned above, Lyttelton proposed to choose a wife for Thomson in 1747; and he apparently wrote his popular religious tract, *Observations on the Conversion and Apostleship of St. Paul* (1747), with the view of making Thomson into a more orthodox Christian. After Thomson's death, Lyttelton busied himself to have *Coriolanus* produced under the most favorable circumstances in January, 1749. The strength of his feeling of proprietorship in Thomson can be seen in the extensive tampering he engaged in for the 1750 edition of the poet's works, and the even more far-reaching "correcting and amending" he desired to introduce in subsequent editions.[105] Under a crumbling and corrupt patronage system in which it was unfortunately necessary for most poets to have a "great friend" to survive, Lyttelton served Thomson reasonably well. But the price was great; and his use of Thomson for political propaganda, his officious meddling in the poet's life and writing, and especially his assumption of the right to manipulate the posthumous publication of the poet's works add up to a bad bargain. The contemplation of Thomson's lifelong courting of patrons is an unpleasant experience; perhaps the best that can be said is that he was in part the victim of a bad system which ignobly reduced most writers very quickly to a state of servile dependence; proud and stubborn geniuses like Samuel Johnson, who resisted the patronage system, were all too rare in the eighteenth century. Thomson, with the aid of the bookseller Andrew Millar, resisted better than most.

Thomson had completed *Coriolanus* by 1747, but failed to have it produced because of a dispute between David Garrick and Thomson over who should act the lead role. Thomson insisted that Coriolanus should be played by his good friend James Quin, whereas Garrick apparently insisted on the part for himself. The play eventually was staged on January 13, 1749, with Quin in the title role. Thomson's last publication during his lifetime was *The Castle of Indolence,* issued by Millar on May 7, 1748. This poem, which was well-received from the beginning and which is in some respects the best of his works, will be discussed in chapter 4. Thomson's close friend and best biographer Patrick Murdoch gives an account of his unexpected death in August of 1748:

> He had always been a timorous horseman; and more so, in a road where numbers of giddy or unskilful riders are continually passing: so that when the weather did not invite him to go by water, he would commonly walk the distance between *London* and *Richmond,* with any acquaintance that offered; with whom he might chat and rest himself, or perhaps dine, by the way. One summer evening, being alone, in his walk from town to *Hammersmith,* he had overheated himself, and in that condition, imprudently took a boat to carry him to *Kew;* apprehending no bad consequence from the chill air on the river, which his walk to his house, at the upper end of *Kew-lane,* had always hitherto prevented. But, now, the cold had so seized him, that next day he found himself in a high fever, so much the more to be dreaded that he was of a full habit. This however, by the use of proper medicines, was removed, so that he was thought to be out of danger:

> till the fine weather having tempted him to expose himself once more to the evening dews, his fever returned with violence, and with such symptoms as left no hopes of a cure. Two days had passed before his relapse was known in town; at last Mr. *Mitchell* and Mr. *Reid*, with Dr. *Armstrong*, being informed of it, posted out at midnight to his assistance: but alas! came only to endure a sight of all others the most shocking to nature, the last agonies of their beloved friend. This lamented death happened on 27th day of *August*, 1748.[106]

His remains were interred in the church at Richmond on August 29.

Thomson was an amiable, gentle man whose death was sincerely mourned by his friends. The following remark in a letter written by Dr. John Armstrong to Murdoch on August 30 is characteristic of the sorrow expressed by the poet's intimate friends: "This blow makes a hideous gap; and the loss of such an agreeable Friend turns some of the sweetest scenes in England into a something waste and desolate; at least for the time: it will be so for a long time with me; for I question whether I shall ever be able to see Richmond again without sorrow and mortification." Millar, who was prostrate, wrote to John Forbes on September 10 that not only "all his friends" but "even those that did not know him" were in grief for Thomson.[107] George Anne Bellamy, an itinerant actress employed at Covent Garden at the time of Thomson's death, wrote many years later in her memoirs: "His death seemed to throw an universal gloom over every susceptible mind. Whilst some lamented the loss of his great poetical talents, all wept for the removal of so good a man. The softness of his manners, his unbounded philanthropy, and indeed the possession of every valuable quality that can adorn a human being, endeared him to every one who had the happiness to be acquainted with him."[108] Memorials were immediately raised by Lyttelton at Hagley Park and by William Shenstone at the Leasowes. Among the memorial poems published was *Musidorus: A Poem Sacred to the Memory of Mr. James Thomson*, by Robert Shiels, a Scotsman who was to publish the first extended account of Thomson's life and work in 1753. But it was left to the young poet William Collins, who had lived for a while near Thomson at Richmond and was now tragically near his final mental breakdown, to publish a really distinguished tribute in his "Ode on the Death of Mr. Thomson" in 1749. Patrick Murdoch, citing "the dirge-like melancholy it breathes, and the warmth of affection that seems to have dictated it,"[109] included the "Ode" in the handsome quarto edition of Thomson's works in 1762 and thus set a pattern of habitually printing Collins' poem as a preface to uncounted editions of *The Seasons* for a hundred years. The "Ode" is a fitting and dignified tribute to one of the most beloved of English poets.

CHAPTER 2

The Seasons

THE Seasons is a long blank verse poem consisting of five separate parts: *Spring, Summer, Autumn, Winter,* and *A Hymn on the Seasons.* Although in the course of many revisions and expansions over twenty years it became somewhat diffuse in its concerns, *The Seasons* is primarily a poem about nature and the impact of nature on the sensations, imagination, intellect, and moral character of man. It is thus both a "descriptive" and a "philosophical" poem. The dominant "theme" of *The Seasons* is the search for knowledge and understanding of the divine harmony assumed to be present in the bewildering and apparently contradictory array of faces which nature presents to man. The impulses and backgrounds for *The Seasons* are various, including prominently (1) the "physicotheological" urge to discover God primarily in his works; (2) Shaftesburian "enthusiasm" and benevolence; (3) Newtonian science; (4) the ancient but popular concept of the Chain of Being; (5) Virgil's *Georgics;* (6) Milton's influence; (7) the Psalms and the Book of Job; (8) Longinus and the concept of the "sublime"; and (9) an expanded awareness of geography. *The Seasons* is a loosely structured poem, and Thomson repeatedly revised and expanded it between the first appearance of *Winter* in 1726 and the final version of *The Seasons* in 1746. There is in existence a very substantial amount of criticism of *The Seasons,* much of it conflicting head-on in its evaluations of Thomson's purposes and achievements. In an introductory book, which must seek some balance in its account of Thomson's larger poetic and dramatic career, I cannot hope to deal with all the problems and critical arguments surrounding *The Seasons.* I shall attempt, nevertheless, to aid the reader's understanding by considering briefly in this chapter (1) the contents of each seasonal part; (2) the problem of fusing successfully the descriptive passages with didactic purposes; (3) the themes and backgrounds of *The Seasons;* (4) the problem of structure or unity in a poem of such diverse subject matter; (5) the style of the poem; and (6) the problem of revision. A discussion of Thomson's elegy on Newton, which is close to *The Seasons* in theme, style, and purpose, will also be included in this chapter.

I Spring

Spring, which since the first collected edition of 1730 has stood first in *The Seasons,* was published in 1728 after both *Winter* (1726) and *Summer* (1727) had appeared. Although it later underwent substantial revision, the overall length did not expand greatly. Version A (1728) had 1082 lines; version B (1730) had 1087; version C (1744) had 1173; and version D (1746) had 1176. The poems in *The Seasons* have been accused of being without structure, but Thomson did adopt a "Chain of Being" order for *Spring:* "The Season is described as it affects the various parts of nature, ascending from the lower to the higher" (3).[1] The choice of this ancient analogy for harmony and order is appropriate to the presentation of spring as a time when the elements of nature are most in harmony. The coming of "gentle Spring" brings soft showers, "Not such as wintry storms on mortals shed,/Oppressing life; but lovely, gentle, kind" (ll. 152–53). Thomson finds an appropriate parallel for the loveliness of Spring in the popular fable of a past golden age when "uncorrupted man" lived happily amid "Harmonious Nature." The beauty and plenitude of vegetable nature in spring are seen primarily in descriptions and catalogs of "unnumbered flowers." Love and harmony in animal life are well illustrated by the "music unconfined" of amorous birds of spring, "prodigal of harmony." To the "curious" who would know the source of such harmony, variety, and beauty, Thomson replies:

> What, but God?
> Inspiring God! who, boundless spirit all
> And unremitting energy, pervades,
> Adjusts, sustains, and agitates the whole.
> He ceaseless works alone, and yet alone
> Seems not to work; with such perfection framed
> Is this complex, stupendous scheme of things.
>
> (ll. 852–58)

The beauty and harmony of spring are to affect man by softening his heart to religious and benevolent concerns:

> Pure Serenity apace
> Induces thought, and contemplation still.
> By swift degrees the love of nature works,
> And warms the bosom; till at last, sublimed
> To rapture and enthusiastic heat,
> We feel the present Deity, and taste
> The joy of God to see a happy world!
>
> (ll. 897–903)

Thomson added to *Spring* in 1744 a specific illustration of this "benevolent man" in harmony with nature, God, and his fellowmen (ll. 904–62). His patron George Lyttelton is seen at Hagley Park, "Planning with warm benevolence of mind/And honest zeal, unwarped by party-rage,/Britannia's weal" (ll. 928–30).

Thomson's scheme of describing the happiness and harmony caused by the "love inclinations" of spring among the flowers, birds, and bees flounders badly when he comes to describe the sexual urges aroused by spring in men. Whereas flowers unblushingly spread their "father-dust" and the birds happily pair off to obey "Nature's great command," men must be more cautious. When the virgin's "wishing bosom heaves/With palpitations wild" (ll. 968–69), she must resist and "Be greatly cautious of . . . betraying man" (ll. 974, 982). Love becomes not the inspirer of harmony and happiness but the source of disorder and torment in a long "tortured lover" passage (ll. 1004–73) in which the "love-dejected" swain suffers and dreamily indulges his "sick imagination." Thomson's radical departure here from his larger scheme in *Spring* is not only an awkward obeisance to the social conventions which men but not birds must heed, but also a poignantly autobiographical portrait of himself as a tortured, rejected lover. To close *Spring,* he returns to his happy and ideal picture by portraying a couple who achieve a perfectly harmonious marital and family life.

II Summer

Summer, first published in 1727, was the second of Thomson's seasonal poems. It underwent extensive revision and expansion by 1746. Version A (1727) had 1146 lines; version B (1730) had 1206; version C (1744) had 1796; and version D (1746) had 1805. Again, there is a structural principle adopted in following the summer's day from sunrise through evening and night. Whereas spring is gentle and feminine, summer is powerful and masculine, symbolized by the "potent sun," darting the "burning influence" of "tyrant Heat" on all below. The plenitude of nature in summer appears in the "Ten thousand forms, ten thousand different tribes" of insects which "People the blaze" (ll. 249–50). Such hordes remind the poet that "Full Nature swarms with life" (l. 289):

> The flowery leaf
> Wants not its soft inhabitants. Secure
> Within its winding citadel the stone
> Holds multitudes. But chief the forest boughs,
> That dance unnumbered to the playful breeze,
> The downy orchard, and the melting pulp
> Of mellow fruit the nameless nations feed
> Of evanescent insects. Where the pool
> Stands mantled o'er with green, invisible
> Amid the floating verdure millions stray.
>
> (ll. 296–305)

To marvel thus at the revelations of microscopic vision was commonplace in the early eighteenth century. Such a vision should remind man of just how little he knows of the "mighty chain of beings" and make him humbly conscious of his limited awareness:

> Has any seen
> The mighty chain of beings, lessening down
> From infinite perfection to the brink
> Of dreary nothing, desolate abyss!
> From which astonished thought recoiling turns?
> Till then, alone let zealous praise ascend
> And hymns of holy wonder to that Power
> Whose wisdom shines as lovely on our minds
> As on our smiling eyes his servant-sun.
>
> (ll. 333–41)

In *Summer,* Thomson emphasizes awe-inspiring aspects of nature, its power and sublimity. To better achieve this purpose, he devotes much of the poem to the torrid zone, where the "raging" aspects of nature ("scorching suns," "prodigious rivers," ferocious beasts, savages, "raging elements") are seen in their most powerful and destructive forms. Closer home again, the awesome power of nature is seen in a thunderstorm, which shatters and blasts trees, cattle, and men. The virtuous and innocent maiden Amelia is stricken in the arms of her lover Celadon and dashed to the ground "a blackened corse" (l. 1216). A different kind of love story appears in the Damon-Musidora episode, in which Damon, languishing with love for Musidora, accidentally sees her undress and bathe. This scene is highly sensual and is clearly suggested by the young Guyon's experience in Spenser's "Bower of Bliss."[2]

The Seasons contains many passages with political or patriotic implications; and, near the end of *Summer,* the poet-observer's exulting enjoyment of the "goodly prospect" around him leads into a long panegyric on "Happy Britannia." As the summer day declines, so also does the intensity of Thomson's portrait of the heat and glory of summer: "The Sun has lost his rage: his downward orb/ Shoots nothing now but animating warmth/ And vital lustre" (ll. 1371–73). Night comes, and the reverent observer of the evening sky closes his reflections with a paean to "Philosophy," which enables the enlightened man

> to gaze
> Creation through; and, from that full complex
> Of never-ending wonders, to conceive
> Of the Sole Being right, who spoke the word,
> And Nature moved complete.
>
> (ll. 1784–88)

III Autumn

Autumn was the last of the four seasonal poems to be written, and was first published with the collected *Seasons* in 1730. Substantial passages from the first versions of both *Winter* and *Summer* were made part of *Autumn* in 1730. There are fewer separate versions of *Autumn* than of the other parts of *The Seasons,* and it underwent less expansion and revision. Version A (1730) had 1269 lines; version B (1744) had 1375; and version C (1746) had 1373. Fields ready for harvest in autumn remind the poet that "These are thy blessings, Industry, rough power!" And *Autumn* begins with a dull section on the blessings of industry and commerce as civilizing forces. Mention of gleaners following the harvest leads to the story of Palemon and Lavinia, a rewriting of the biblical story of Ruth, with the same happy ending. All is not happy in autumn, however; storm and flood sometimes destroy the crops and ruin "the big hopes/ And well-earned treasures of the painful year" (ll. 342–43). Hunting scenes dominate one section of *Autumn;* and an "after the hunt" feasting and drinking bout is developed in mock-heroic terms:

> Before their maudlin eyes,
> Seen dim and blue, the double tapers dance,
> Like the sun wading through the misty sky.
> Then, sliding soft, they drop. Confused above,
> Glasses and bottles, pipes and gazetteers,
> As if the table even itself was drunk,
> Lie a wet broken scene: and wide, below,
> Is heaped the social slaughter—where astride
> The lubber Power in filthy triumph sits,
> Slumbrous, inclining still from side to side,
> And steeps them drenched in potent sleep till morn.
> (ll. 554-64)

A more gentle and pleasant scene presents a lazy, personified Autumn "basking" in the midst of his fruition:

> And, as I steal along the sunny wall,
> Where Autumn basks, with fruit empurpled deep,
> My pleasing theme continual prompts my thought—
> Presents the downy peach, the shining plum
> With a fine bluish mist of animals
> Clouded, the ruddy nectarine, and dark
> Beneath his ample leaf the luscious fig.
> The vine too here her curling tendrils shoots,
> Hangs out her clusters glowing to the south,
> And scarcely wishes for a warmer sky.
> (ll. 673–82)

Fogs, bird migrations, and "the fading many-coloured woods" are part of the autumn scene. The tribute to "Happy Britannia" in *Summer* is matched by a tribute to Thomson's native Scotland in *Autumn.* A "desolated prospect" in late autumn arouses in the observer a "Philosophic Melancholy." In some manner, this philosophic melancholy arouses "correspondent" social feelings in the observer: "The love of nature unconfined, and, chief,/ Of human race; the large ambitious wish/To make them blest" (ll. 1020–22).

In a lengthy section (ll. 1235–1351) at the end of *Autumn,* Thomson paraphrases Virgil's *Georgics* (bk. 2, ll. 458 ff.) in praise of the rural life in harmony with nature:

Oh! knew he but his happiness, of men
The happiest he! who far from public rage
Deep in the vale, with a choice few retired,
Drinks the pure pleasures of the rural life.

. . . .

Sure peace is his; a solid life, estranged
To disappointment and fallacious hope—
Rich in content, in Nature's bounty rich,
In herbs and fruits. . . .

. . . .

Here too dwells simple truth, plain innocence,
Unsullied beauty, sound unbroken youth
Patient of labour—with a little pleased,
Health ever-blooming, unambitious toil,
Calm contemplation, and poetic ease.

(ll. 1235–38, 1257–60, 1273–77)

IV Winter

Winter was the first part of *The Seasons* to be written. Beginning as a relatively brief "mood" poem in 1726, it later underwent radical expansion and revision and exists in more different versions than any other part of *The Seasons.* Version A (March, 1726) had 405 lines; version B (June, 1726) had 463; version C (quarto, 1730) had 781; version D (octavo, 1730) had 787; version E (1744) had 1069; and version F (1746) had 1069. *Winter,* like *Summer,* deals with the more extreme, "sublime" aspects of nature. Winter humbles man with its "awful" and destructive powers. Not only the subject matter, but also the style of *Winter* is to attempt the sublime: "To swell her [the muse's] note with all the rushing winds,/ To suit her sounding cadence to the floods;/ As is her theme, her numbers wildly great" (ll. 25–27). His "muse" soars as Thomson attempts to grasp the awful majesty of nature and her impact on the poet:

Nature! great parent! whose unceasing hand
Rolls round the Seasons of the changeful year,
How mighty, how majestic are thy works!
With what a pleasing dread they swell the soul,
That sees astonished, and astonished sings!

(ll. 106–10)

Winter is full of storms, described with effective use of strong action words, such as "burst," "hurls," "torrent," "lashed," and "raging":

Then issues forth the storm with sudden burst,
And hurls the whole precipitated air
Down in a torrent. On the passive main
Descends the ethereal force, and with strong gust
Turns from its bottom the discoloured deep.
Through the black night that sits immense around,
Lashed into foam, the fierce-conflicting brine
Seems o'er a thousand raging waves to burn.

(ll. 153–60)

The transforming and humbling effect of a heavy snow storm is described: "Earth's universal face, deep-hid and chill,/Is one wild dazzling waste, that buries wide/The works of man" (ll. 238–40). A farmer is overwhelmed by the snowstorm, lost in his own fields. As yet ignorant that their father is "a stiffened corse,"

In vain his little children, peeping out
Into the mingling storm, demand their sire
With tears of artless innocence. Alas!
Nor wife nor children more shall he behold,
Nor friends, nor sacred home.

(ll. 313–17)

But nature, always paradoxical, has another side in winter. "Rustic mirth" gladdens the winter fireside. Winter is "ruin," says Thomson, to only the "thoughtless eye." Winter exerts a renewing and invigorating force on nature, "Killing infectious damps, and the spent air/Storing afresh with elemental life" (ll. 695–96). Winter "animates our blood" and "Refines our spirits" (ll. 699–700).

As Thomson's muse in *Summer* had flown away to the torrid zone in search of more extreme forms of the "scorching" and "raging" aspects of nature, in *Winter* he visits the "frigid zone," in order to be "astonished" at the greater relentlessness of winter there (ll. 794 ff). This is the permanent abode of Winter, from which he sallies forth periodically to oppress other parts of the world:

Here Winter holds his unrejoicing court;
And through his airy hall the loud misrule
Of driving tempest is for ever heard:
Here the grim tyrant meditates his wrath;
Here arms his winds with all-subduing frost;
Moulds his fierce hail, and treasures up his snows,
With which he now oppresses half the globe.

(ll. 895–901)

Finally, the "trickling thaw" signals the passing of winter; and with the coming of early spring the seasonal cycle of nature which Thomson has followed through gentle spring, glorious summer, fruitful autumn, and destructive winter is on the threshold of beginning anew. But the passage of winter into spring suggests also to Thomson the passing of time into eternity. "Wintry time," with its "bounded view" of nature and reality, will pass into the "unbounded Spring" of eternity:

> Ye good distressed!
> Ye noble few! who here unbending stand
> Beneath life's pressure, yet bear up a while,
> And what your bounded view, which only saw
> A little part, deemed evil is no more:
> The storms of wintry time will quickly pass,
> And one unbounded Spring encircle all.
>
> (ll. 1063–69)

V A Hymn on the Seasons

The concluding *Hymn* was first added to the collected *Seasons* in 1730. It was later revised only slightly and expanded not at all, the original 121 lines being reduced to 118 before 1746. The hymn is intended to be a crowning expression of the theme of the revelation of God in his works and of the gloriousness of the creator of such a "sublime" nature. The hymn is addressed to God and begins, "These, as they change, Almighty Father! these/ Are but the varied God." The "beauty" of spring, "glory" of summer, "bounty" of autumn, and "awful" aspects of winter are attributes of God seen in nature. Such magnificence and mystery can invite us only to hymns of praise and wonder. These ideas share in, but transcend, the widespread physico-theological theories of Thomson's day, which were using recent advances in science to look for evidence of God's handiwork in every flower, leaf, and stem. But Thomson's *Hymn* has more in common with Psalm 148, in which all earthly creatures are called upon to praise God, and with the morning hymn of Adam and Eve in *Paradise Lost* (V, 153–208). Thomson's *Hymn,* and *The Seasons,* end with the vision that the "seeming evil" of man's present state will become fully clear in future worlds. Man on earth, however, faced with the majesty and mystery of God as revealed in nature, must finally fall back on "expressive Silence" as an act of praise.

VI *Description and Didacticism*

In the later eighteenth and nineteenth centuries, Thomson was judged, and given high marks, in "descriptive" nature poetry. Moreover, it is probably true that twentieth-century readers of *The Seasons,* coming to the poem with expectations colored by long familiarity with the habits and values of nineteenth-century English and American poetry, will find most congenial Thomson's imaginative descriptions of nature and mild adumbrations of "Romanticism." But the entire critical and popular tradition portraying Thomson as the sweetest of descriptive bards and earliest of the "preromantics" is at best one-sided and at worst distorts completely the pattern and intention of the poem.

Most attempts to describe the nature and purpose of *The Seasons* have paid too little attention to Thomson's own remarks in the preface to the second edition of *Winter* (1726). Thomson here spells out unambiguously his reasons for choosing nature as his subject. Echoing Addison's three sources of the "Pleasures of the Imagination," he cites the variety, beauty, and magnificence of nature.[3] But the mere description or survey of these attributes of nature is not the primary subject, but rather human response to them. This response is described several times by Thomson in a three-fold manner: "to awake the poetical enthusiasm, the philosophical reflection, and the moral sentiment." In other terms, nature is to "amuse the fancy, enlighten the head, and warm the heart." That Thomson considered this an important point worth making is indicated by yet a third repetition of the idea in the same essay, where he associates with poetry "the most charming power of imagination, the most exalting force of thought, the most affecting touch of sentiment." The identical order in which the imaginative, intellectual, and moral responses are mentioned in each instance suggests an ascending hierarchy of significant responses to nature.

Joseph Addison, whose "Pleasures of the Imagination" papers in the *Spectator* are the best preparation for understanding *The Seasons,* had distinguished the three faculties of sensation, imagination, and reason. The grossest of these is sensation; the most refined is reason or "understanding." Between the two lies "imagination" or "fancy." Addison did not of course create this scheme; but his expression and interpretation of it was widely influential and quite familiar to Thomson, who wrote of this hierarchy of faculties in *Summer:* "Each to his rank, from plain perception up/To the fair forms of fancy's fleeting train;/To reason then, deducing truth from truth, /And notion quite abstract" (ll. 1793–96). Thomson, like Addison and the eighteenth century generally, followed John Locke in making sensation or "plain perception" the ultimate source of all ideas. The "imagination" or "fancy" could not create, but could re-create or combine "images" received through sense impression. In Thomson's words, fancy

> receives
> The whole magnificence of heaven and earth,
> And every beauty, delicate or bold,
> Obvious or more remote, with livelier sense,
> Diffusive painted on the rapid mind.
> (*Summer,* ll. 1748–52)

Reason, or what Thomson elsewhere calls the "philosophical reflection" or the "force of thought," seeks meaning or truth in the materials of experience. Most importantly in *The Seasons,* reason is engaged in "up-tracing, from the dreary void,/The chain of causes and effects to Him,/The world-producing Essence, who alone/ Possesses being" (*Summer,* ll. 1745–48). But Thomson went a step further and emphasized also another response to nature, the "moral sentiment," or that which "betters" or "warms" the heart. Nature can "enlarge and transport the soul" to prepare it for moral, social, and benevolent concerns.

This combination of imaginative description with passages of philosophical or moral reflection has led modern critics to designate Thomson as one of the most significant pioneers of a type of blank-verse poem common in the eighteenth-century, called variously "descriptive-didactic," "descriptive-reflective," or "descriptive-meditative." The double designation in itself calls attention to the problem of whether the two activities are successfully merged. Joseph Warton in 1756 did not try to find an artistic juxtaposition of elements in *The Seasons,* but found justification for the moral passages in their superiority to mere description: "It is one of the greatest and most pleasing arts of descriptive poetry, to introduce moral sentences and instructions in an oblique and indirect manner, in places where one naturally expects only painting and amusement." We are pleased, he says, "to find a thing where we should never have looked to meet with it."[4] Henry A. Beers remarked in 1899, "To relieve the monotony of a descriptive poem, the author introduced moralizing digressions."[5] Twentieth-century critics have emphasized either "description" or "reflection" in *The Seasons* as one or the other has suited their own sensibilities, interpretations, or critical purposes. Elizabeth Nitchie stated in 1919 that "His fundamental aim was to describe rather than teach." Marjorie Nicolson remarked in 1959 that "Thomson was on the whole content to draw and paint the new, expansive, diversified Nature, rather than to psychologize upon her effect upon the soul of man." Ralph Cohen, on the other hand, stated flatly in 1970 that *The Seasons* is not a "descriptive," but rather a "religious didactic poem."[6]

If Thomson was in accomplishment more successful and influential as a descriptive poet, he was in intention also a philosophical one. Joseph Warton was speaking for the age in remarking, "It may be observed in general, that description of the external beauties of nature, is usually the first effort of a young genius, before he hath studied manners and passions."[7] Thomson's contemporaries received *The Seasons* enthusiastically as the work of a "young genius" and confidently expected him to progress to "manners and passions." In his later career he wrote mediocre tragedies; failed with his long political poem *Liberty;* and included more social, moral, and political concerns in revisions of *The Seasons*. We may accept Robert Shiels' statement in 1753 that "Thomson was born a descriptive poet"[8] and Marjorie Nicolson's verdict in 1946 that "He was, above all, a poet of imagination,"[9] while still regretting that Thomson never quite realized this himself. *The Seasons* presents a pattern of not only imaginative, but also intellectual and moral responses to nature. In Thomson's own words, his descriptions were followed by "suitable Reflections" or were "raised, and animated by moral, and sublime, Reflections." Whatever "pleasures of the imagination" nature might provide, it is of greater significance that "The informing Author in his work appears" (*Spring*, l. 860); and God's magnificent theater of the great, surprising, and beautiful is to be contemplated for the evidence it provides of divine wisdom, benevolence, and harmony and also for the "softening" effect it can have on the moral nature of man.

Thomson certainly did not consider his philosophical and moral passages to be unrelated to, or even apart from, his descriptive sections. The point is that nature is fraught with philosophical and moral meaning; to "the enlightened few,/Whose godlike minds philosophy exalts" (*Summer*, ll. 1714–15), whom Thomson repeatedly distinguished from the "vulgar" or the "fond sequacious herd," nature provides inspiration, evidence, analogies, and emblems which lead to knowledge and moral improvement. In a table of contents to *Spring,* for example, Thomson summarizes one section of the poem as follows: "Influence of the Spring on man, inspiring a universal benevolence, the love of mankind, and of nature. Accounted for from that general harmony which then attunes the world." In *Autumn,* a "desolated prospect" arouses in the observer a "Philosophic Melancholy" which leads to "correspondent passions" in the moral sphere:

> As fast the correspondent passions rise,
> As varied, and as high—devotion raised
> To rapture, and divine astonishment;
> The love of nature unconfined, and, chief,
> Of human race; the large ambitious wish
> To make them blest; the sigh for suffering worth;
> . . . .
> The sympathies of love and friendship dear,
> With all the social offspring of the heart.
>
> (ll. 1017–22, 1028–29)

But the exact quality of the "correspondence" between love of nature and love for the human race remains vague, just as the following effusion from *Summer* leaves unanswered the question of just how "nature's vast Lyceum" or "kind school" manage to affect or interact with social relationships, philosophy, virtue, or friendship:

> Now the soft hour
> Of walking comes for him who lonely loves
> To seek the distant hills, and there converse
> With nature, there to harmonize his heart,
> And in pathetic song to breathe around
> The harmony to others. Social friends,
> Attuned to happy unison of soul—
> To whose exulting eye a fairer world,
> Of which the vulgar never had a glimpse,
> Displays its charms; whose minds are richly fraught
> With philosophic stores, superior light;
> And in whose breast enthusiastic burns
> Virtue, the sons of interest deem romance—
> Now called abroad, enjoy the falling day:
> Now to the verdant portico of woods,
> To nature's vast Lyceum, forth they walk;
> By that kind school where no proud master reigns,
> The full free converse of the friendly heart,
> Improving and improved.
>
> (ll. 1379–97)

At times Thomson managed thematic, analogical, or structural associations between the descriptive and the didactic in *The Seasons;* but at other times he failed to do so convincingly. Earl Wasserman, in his article, "Nature Moralized: The Divine Analogy in the Eighteenth Century,"[10] has provided a sensible explanation for this failure to fuse fact and interpretation successfully. Wasserman starts with the familiar concept that the poet who wrote earlier than the scientific revolution of the seventeenth century had the advantage of "a world of pre-existent poetic materials" already infused with value and significance because ". . . it was assumed that God, expressing Himself in all creation, made the physical, moral, and spiritual levels analogous to each other and to Himself. Therefore, object and subject, thing and value, matter and spirit, were related proportionately; for the divine architect made the universe like man, and man like angel, and all in the image of Himself. All not-objects could be truthfully expressed as like objects" (40). Although the work of science was largely to "fracture" or "enervate" the divine analogy, the eighteenth-century poets yet clung to it. What had existed beneath the level of consciousness in the Elizabethan mind now became an almost overly conscious activity: "No longer thinking analogically, but consciously thinking about thinking analogically, it [the age] had split a unified concept into its two component parts and into two separate but related events. Analogy is no longer a frame of mind for meaningful perception, but a pattern for chronological procedure; metaphor has yielded to simile as the key structural figure, and nature and moral truth belong on different sides of the same equation. Hence the characteristic bipartite structure of the descriptive poetry of [many eighteenth-century poets]" (71).

VII *Themes and Backgrounds*

The Seasons is a poem which attempts to assert the divine harmony of God's world. As such, it is an intensely "religious" poem, although hardly in an orthodox sense. It is a poem embodying an excited search for God's order, harmony, and greatness in nature and seeking to explain the impact of nature on man, represented primarily as a softening of his heart to benevolence and love for his fellowman and to social concerns which find their broadest expression in patriotism. At its best, *The Seasons* departs from the more typical Augustan poetic practice of summarizing or generalizing neatly about human experience. Although Thomson's habitual practice is to move from particulars to general statements, he is at his best in writing the passages of enthusiastic observation which provide the raw materials for his sometimes feeble generalizations. *The Seasons* is at its most successful an exclamation rather than an intellectual argument. Utilizing generally the present tense rather than the past tense, the speaker or "I" of the poem is represented as engaged in an enthusiastic search for knowledge. In his attempt to understand the mystery, multiplicity, awesomeness, and beauty of God's creation, he observes, catalogs, and exclaims; climbs heights in an attempt to see larger and broader patterns; is overwhelmed and withdraws to "retreats" in order to reflect on the bewildering multiplicity of sensations which nature has "flung" at his "straining eye"; "flies away" with his muse to the torrid and the polar zones in a search for more awesome sights and sounds; utilizes the "new science" to help him understand the mysteries of natural phenomena; and, when science proves inadequate, falls back on desperate acts of the imagination to "lay the mountains bare, and wide display/Their hidden structure to the astonished view" (*Autumn,* ll. 779–80) in order to perceive "The full-adjusted harmony of things" (*Autumn,* l. 835).

The powers of the "philosophic mind" to translate the overwhelming variety, beauty, and awesomeness of nature into some coherent system finally and absolutely understood are limited, however. Even Newton, who was revered almost as a deity because of the powers of his mind, could not fully explain the mysteries. For man's limited vision, it is finally "faith" which assures him that nature is formed and infused by "boundless love and perfect wisdom" (*Summer,* l. 1804). This faith, however, could hardly be described as conventional Christian faith that divine grace can redeem man from evil. It is rather an intellectualized faith in the rightness and rationality of the universe, a faith that only a lack of knowledge prevents man from seeing the fitness of things. A typical follower of Newton, Thomson considered the strenuous search for knowledge and meaning in nature, which is finally impenetrable, yet exceedingly appropriate and rewarding because we are only in an "infancy of being" which will continue into an immortality typically conceived of by Newton's followers not as a fixed mystical state but as an ever-widening circle of knowledge and understanding. After Newton's death, he was imagined by his enthusiastic admirers to be ecstatically exploring new wonders in his angelic state: "mounted on cherubic Wing,/Thy swift Career is with the whirling Orbs,/

Comparing Things with Things, in Rapture lost,/And grateful Adoration."[11]

Along with his extreme reverence for Newton, who even in this "dim Spot" of earth "Could trace the secret Hand of PROVIDENCE,/ Wide-working thro' this universal Frame,"[12] Thomson was also influenced in his attitude toward nature by the "enthusiast" third earl of Shaftesbury's *Characteristics,* a pervasive background with which Thomson had been intimately familiar since his youth. In fact, the spirit of parts of Thomson's *Seasons* is remarkably well described by this passage from Shaftesbury:

> O glorious nature! supremely fair and sovereignly good! all-loving and all-lovely, all-divine! whose looks are so becoming and of such infinite grace; whose study brings such wisdom, and whose contemplation such delight; whose every single work affords an ampler scene, and is a nobler spectacle than all which ever art presented! O mighty Nature! wise substitute of Providence! impowered creatress! Or thou impowering Deity, supreme creator! Thee I invoke and thee alone adore. . . .
>
> Thy being is boundless, unsearchable, impenetrable. In thy immensity all thought is lost, fancy gives over its flight, and wearied imagination spends itself in vain, finding no coast nor limit of this ocean. . . . Thus having oft essayed, thus sallied forth into the wide expanse, when I return again within myself, struck with the sense of this so narrow being and of the fulness of that immense one, I dare no more behold the amazing depths nor sound the abyss of Deity.
>
> Yet since by thee, O sovereign mind, I have been formed such as I am, intelligent and rational, since the peculiar dignity of my nature is to know and contemplate thee, permit that with due freedom I exert those faculties with which thou hast adorned me. Bear with my venturous and bold approach.[13]

The Seasons is a religious poem, but the nature of Thomson's religion has been variously interpreted. He has been called "unquestionably" and "definitely" a deist,[14] but a recent extensive discussion of *The Seasons* emphasizes throughout Thomson's "orthodox view" and his "traditional Christian view."[15] Furthermore, *The Seasons* was long considered valuable for its inspiration to moral and religious reflection. The Reverend J. Evans edited *The Seasons* in 1802 with the hope that "the trouble now taken, may conduce to promote the virtue and piety of the Rising Generation."[16] But to call Thomson either a "deist" or "orthodox" is misleading. He was not a deist, i.e., one who openly maintained that unaided human reason can find in natural phenomena an adequate notion of God without the aid of revelation and who typically thought of God as "First

Cause" removed from his creation and operating in it only by second causes. For Thomson recognized the inadequacy of reason, at least in our present "infancy of being"; and he spoke of an immanent God who "fills, sustains, and actuates the Whole," who "sustains and animates the whole," and who "pervades, sustains,/ Surrounds and fills this universal Frame."[17] Neither is this pantheism, for God also "dwells awfully retired/ From mortal eye or angel's purer ken" (*Summer,* ll. 177–78). Thus Thomson is "orthodox" to the extent of avoiding Deism on the one hand and pantheism (equating God with Nature) on the other. Nevertheless, it requires quite an effort of imagination to see Thomson, and also many of his "Christian" contemporaries, as "orthodox." Under the influence of the rational systems of his day, Thomson departed significantly from the strict Presbyterianism of his youth. His patron George Lyttelton was deeply troubled after Thomson's death that his friend had not openly professed the Christian faith. In *The Seasons,* supernatural revelation is absent; and what man cannot learn about God by applying his reason to natural phenomena he is to learn in a future state conceived of as increased understanding of the perfect pattern of things now seen as imperfect because our reason and knowledge are not as good as they will be in a future state. The basic orthodox idea of salvation through Christ or grace is absent from and foreign to the emphasis of *The Seasons.* There is a tacit denial of the Fall of Man in the emphasis on the "full perfection" of nature and also on a "moral world . . . fitted and impelled/ By wisdom's finest hand, and issuing all/ In general good" (*Winter,* ll. 583, 585–87). And certainly it is hardly orthodox to attribute "evil" only to our present "bounded view" of God's perfect creation.

Thomson's age was filled with physico-theologians, Newtonians, and Latitudinarians, all of whom found themselves, in spite of their common clamor against the godlessness of deists and atheists, sharing to some extent the deistic emphasis on the marvelous rightness and regularity of the world and on the powers of man's reason to ascertain it. Against the background of seventeenth-century rational and scientific thought and achievement, the theological trend after 1660 was toward the belief that man's "natural light," properly applied, was more important to religious truth than revelation. Even when this trend of thought did not lead to Unitarianism, Deism, or atheism, it strongly tinctured with rationalism the more "orthodox." The decline of belief in revelation was accompanied by tendencies to identify religion with morality and to de-emphasize the Fall. While continuing to defend revelation in order to keep themselves out of the deist camp, such pillars of the age as John Locke, Archbishop John Tillotson, Samuel Clarke, and Joseph Addison were yet thoroughgoing rationalists. Thomson and Addison are alike in their readiness to grasp new ideas. Both were eclectic in their religious philosophies; both the *Spectator* and *The Seasons* harbor statements which are not "orthodox" and of which their authors were perhaps not fully aware of the implications.

Thomson's purpose in *The Seasons* of showing how "The informing Author in his works appears" (*Spring,* l. 860) is part of a widespread "physico-theological" urge in the early eighteenth century. Many influential books, including John Ray's *Wisdom of God Manifested in the Works of the Creation* (1691) and William Derham's *Physico-Theology* (1713), sought to prove the existence of God and of a beneficent Providence operating in the world not by revelation but by citing evidence from nature, God's handiwork. The argument from design is of course very old, but it acquired new force in a rational age which had at hand striking and abundant new evidence provided by the scientific advances of the seventeenth century. Our later notion of a "conflict" between science and religion was unheard-of; and scientific study of this sort was looked upon as going hand in hand with religion to refute the materialists and atheists who were reviving the ancient doctrines of Democritus, Epicurus, and Lucretius, which denied purpose or design in nature and attributed everything to chance. Addison spoke for the age when he remarked, "The Supream Being has made the best Arguments for his own Existence, in the Formation of the Heavens and the Earth."[18] Thomson's enthusiastic concern to discover in nature the "all-perfect Hand/That poised, impels, and rules the steady whole" (*Summer,* ll. 41–42) is very much a part of this physico-theological tradition.

Thomson also shared a climate of opinion which is sometimes called "Newtonianism." Newton was Thomson's hero, to whom he addressed an enthusiastic elegy in 1727. Maren-Sofie Röstvig has aptly remarked: "Newton's vision of the universe seemed to Thomson the supreme achievement of humanity, the magic moment towards which the whole of history had tended from the earliest days. Thomson's own poetry is best understood as an effort to describe Newton's vision, but on a strictly *poetic* level. . . . Thomson attempted to convey a poet's impression of the whole scheme of things."[19] The growing seventeenth-century belief in the empirical process of investigation had been given its greatest justification in the triumph of Newton's system. Thomson the "Newtonian" poet shared with the scientists the view that "All the strangeness, the mystery, of man's universe must yield sooner or later to the powers of reason."[20] If the romantic poets were later to lament keenly this reduction of the mystery and loveliness of nature to rule and line, the case was otherwise with such a poet as Thomson. That the rainbow or the comet has lost its mystery and awe for the "philosophic mind" is the source, not of loss of beauty or wonder, but of vastly increased pleasure and admiration for God's perfect and regular scheme of things. Newton "with awful Wing pursu'd / The COMET thro' the long Elliptic Curve,"[21] with the result that, even though the "fond sequacious herd" see the comet with "superstitious horrors,"

> . . . the enlightened few,
> Whose godlike minds philosophy exalts,
> The glorious stranger hail. They feel a joy
> Divinely great; they in their powers exult,
> That wondrous force of thought, which mounting spurns
> This dusky spot, and measures all the sky;
> While, from his far excursions through the wilds
> Of barren ether, faithful to his time,
> They see the blazing wonder rise anew.
>
> (*Summer,* ll. 1714–22)

Nevertheless, though this rapturous portrayal of the philosophic mind reducing God's nature to a few simple laws is characteristic of *The Seasons,* two further observations need to be made. The first is that the Newtonian scientists and most of the poets who celebrated them recognized clearly the limitations of human reason in its present state and typically represented man's immortality as an ever-widening awareness and knowledge of the perfection of God's works. Hence Thomson's "system" of which he wrote to his Scottish friend William Cranstoun in 1735: "This, I think, we may be sure of: that a future State must be better than this; and so on thro the never-ceasing Succession of future States; every one rising upon the last, an everlasting new Display of infinite Goodness! But hereby hangs a System, not calculated perhaps for the Meridian where you live tho' for that of your own Mind, and too long to be explained in a Letter."[22] The second observation is that neither Newton nor most of his followers ever represented the universe as a perfect "machine" from which God has removed himself as an essential presence. Gravity itself was a mysterious, unexplainable force, sometimes interpreted as the direct hand of God in nature. Also, as the regular mechanical laws of nature became more obvious to the seventeenth-century scientists and philosophers, they preserved God's presence in the universe by identifying it with absolute space. Newton, in a famous definition, called space the "Sensorium" of God, implying that in spatial infinity God perceives everything perfectly, just as men perceive imperfectly with eye or mind that which lies immediately around them. In a way, this was to submerge the supernatural God into nature; but at least it was not a nature without God, a machine of which God was only the "First Contriver." Rather God, as Thomson states, "pervades, sustains,/Surrounds and fills the universal Frame."[23]

If some poetry, such as that of Donne, can be called poetry of the microcosm, in which the greater world is reduced to whatever significance it may have for the speaker's own "little world": "She's all states, and all princes I," Thomson's poetry, on the other hand, is poetry of the macrocosm, the "mighty maze" to which he must adjust and in which he must seek meaning. As a basic analogy for his representation of the macrocosm, Thomson utilized the ancient conception of the universe as a Chain of Being, which A. O. Lovejoy reminds us attained its "widest diffusion and acceptance" in the eighteenth century.[24] This conception is also belabored in Addison's *Spectator* papers, Pope's *Essay on Man,* and numerous other works of the period. Thomson refers several times to "The mighty chain of beings, lessening down/From infinite perfection to the brink/Of dreary nothing, desolate abyss!" (*Summer,* ll. 334–36). In *Spring,* he adopts the chain of being as an organizational principle, tracing the influence of spring "on inanimate matter, on vegetables, on brute animals, and last on Man." Typically for his age, he extols the microscopic discoveries which had opened man's eyes to the multitudinous forms of life farther down the scale, peopling every leaf, stone, and drop of water. As always, however, Thomson also emphasizes man's present inability to comprehend fully the entire scale. Even the marvelous "microscopic eye" cannot see down the scale as far as "dreary nothing"; and for man a cloud also "sits deep," obscuring the "world of spirits" which exist in the ascending scale above man. The characteristics of nature typically emphasized in *The Seasons* are all related to, or a part of, the primary Chain of Being concept: plenitude (the sheer overflowing fulness of nature); order and harmony; and the seemingly infinite variety or "gradation" of nature.

In his desire to include as much observation of God's beautiful, awe-inspiring, and surprising theater of nature as possible, Thomson is expansive and inclusive. The speaker-wanderer or "I" of the poem shifts his perspective, mood, or mode of expression frequently as he observes, describes, and catalogs the materials of nature in an attempt to include as much of the "whole scheme of things" as possible. In *Mountain Gloom and Mountain Glory,* Marjorie Nicolson calls the genre of *The Seasons,* Mallet's *Excursion,* and Savage's *The Wanderer* the "excursion" poem, remarking that "The 'excursion' poets of the eighteenth century rose upon 'wings sublime,' soared into the Newtonian heavens, then descended to earth where they flew to different lands, plumbed the depths of ocean, and dived 'beneath the darksome caverns' into the secret places, constantly reiterating their 'delight,' 'wonder,' 'awe,' and 'astonishment' at the variety and profusion of a Nature made in the image of an exuberant Deity. As they flew or swooped or dived, they philosophized, seeking natural rather than supernatural explanations for fossils and gems, meteors, storms, earthquake, thunder and lightning, volcanic eruptions" (331). Of Thomson specifically she adds, "The canvas of *The Seasons* is so extensive that it includes, as Thomson intended, nearly all the phenomena of Nature at various seasons, at various times of day and night" (353).

In addition to Newton, Shaftesbury, and the physico-theologians, many other background influences are apparent in *The Seasons.* Although a discussion of these influences would make a book in itself, it is essential to indicate some of the major ones at least briefly. Among the literary influences, Virgil's *Georgics* is paramount in importance. In an age of literary "kinds," Thomson's poem was recognized as being "of the Georgic kind," combining description with didacticism on an extensive scale and permeated with echoes and paraphrases of the *Georgics.* The extent and nature of this influence of the *Georgics* on *The Seasons* have been much discussed by others;[25] suffice it to say here that in adapting and modifying the "Georgic" kind for his *Seasons,* Thomson was insuring the dignity of his endeavor. A didactic form, the Georgic was the "poem that ran deepest in the blood stream of Pope's age";[26] it was a much loftier "form" than pastoral or ode and provided a ready model for Thomson's effort to combine his "devotion to the works of Nature" with didacticism and patriotism. As Dwight Durling has remarked, "The essential motifs of the *Georgics* reappear in *The Seasons:* the glorification of labor and the life of the husbandman through their associations with patriotism, morality, religion, and the beauties of nature" (46). Along with the *Georgics,* another primary model for the "sublime" concerns, exalted conceptions, and elevated style of *The Seasons* is Milton's *Paradise Lost,* in which Thomson also found the primary inspiration for his blank verse. Also, the cadences, moods, and images of Milton's "L'Allegro," and "Il Penseroso" are frequently to be found in *The Seasons.* As previously mentioned, the Book of Job and the Psalms from the Old Testament also provided Thomson a model for his exalted descriptions of God's handiwork in nature. The primary influences of Virgil, Milton, and the Bible all merge with the impact of Longinus and his concept of the "sublime," which encouraged "sweeping, lofty, harmonious, emotional concerns"[27] in eighteenth-century poetry.

Other influences include John Philips' *Cyder* (1708), Pope's *Windsor Forest* (1713), and Gay's *Rural Sports* (1713, 1720), all of which lurk in Thomson's consciousness as he follows these writers in the "Georgic" tradition. Thomson's use of the four seasons as a framework for his poem may have been suggested by William Hinchliffe's *Seasons* (1718), or by Pope's *Pastorals* (1709). There are also interesting echoes in *The Seasons* of Charles Cotton's *Poems on Several Occasions* (1689). In addition, well established traditions of the pastoral poem and of the topographical or "local" poem overlap with the Georgic tradition in accounting for the basic elements of a poem like *The Seasons.* Spenser, Shakespeare, Blackmore, Locke, Addison, and Lucretius are among the many other writers who are present to one degree or another in *The Seasons.* A. D. McKillop and Horace E. Hamilton have pointed out the significant extent to which Thomson's wide reading in travel books, geographies, books on gardening and husbandry, and scientific works also influenced his writing of *The Seasons.*[28] Thomson's knowledge of painting and sculpture was extensive; and the impact of these arts on his poetry has been widely and variously interpreted.

Two facts should be emphasized at this point. First, even such an incomplete list as this should suggest that Thomson was not the rebel against tradition that some literary histories have presented him. In an important sense, *The Seasons* is a "traditional" poem, reflecting its author's knowledge of and respect for the best literature of the past. On the other hand, he was not simply an imitator, but was able to mold his rich materials into something new and original.

VIII *Structure*

Robert Shiels, one of Thomson's earliest critics, noted in 1753 that *The Seasons* "seems written without a plan"; and Samuel Johnson, who was following Shiels at least in part when he wrote his "Life of Thomson" in 1781, remarked that "The great defect of *The Seasons* is want of method."[29] In 1778, however, John Aikin elaborately defended *The Seasons* as a unified and "comprehensive whole";[30] and Percival Stockdale, reacting in 1793 to what he called Johnson's "absolute nonsense," insisted that "It has all the order, and method that any sensible, and liberal critic; that any reader, except a dry, formal pedant, could wish."[31] Thus began a critical argument which has continued to the present day. In 1806, a critic in the *Edinburgh Review* called "that singular incoherency which pervades the whole poem" a "radical defect";[32] and B. Ifor Evans and Patricia Spacks have in the twentieth century called *The Seasons,* respectively, an "odd medley" and "a thing of shreds and patches."[33] But Mrs. Spacks also admits that "It may be treated to some extent as a coherent whole, a totality possessing organized form, despite many aspects which seriously lessen the possibility of unity"; and Ralph Cohen, in *The Unfolding of The Seasons* (1970), has strenuously defended Thomson's artistry, which, he maintains, includes deft handling of the kind or degree of "unity" which Thomson found appropriate to his purposes. Pertinent also to the problem of "structure" or "unity" in *The Seasons* is an essay by Peter Thorpe, in which he argues persuasively that "some of its [eighteenth-century poetry, including *The Seasons*] most esteemed examples succeed without unity, structure, coherence, pattern, or (to use the chief Augustan word for structure) *design,* and . . . such lack of unity does not detract from the beauty and force of the poetry."[34] Denying the pertinence of attempting to find "unity" in such poems as *The Seasons* or Cowper's *The Task,* Thorpe finds the "essential source of their beauty" in "their rich variety and unpredictable flights" (249). D. J. Greene finds in *The Seasons* and in Cowper's *The Task* a "frank impressionism" which delights in "'faggoting notions as they fall'" rather than anything which can be called logical structure.[35]

Certainly James Sutherland errs in placing *The Seasons* among those eighteenth-century works whose "poetical structure is not held together by emotional stresses and strains, but by a sort of steel framework of intellectual argument."[36] For *The Seasons,* if it holds together at all, is not held together by "intellectual" consistency or by a logical progression of its "argument." The best parts of this "sublime" poem are exclamatory and connected emotionally or associatively if at all. Ralph Cohen has argued more successfully for a "stylistic" and "thematic" unity in *The Seasons,* pointing out Thomson's extensive use of "repetitive themes, images, words" as a unifying device in the poem. I do not wish to repeat Cohen's complex and detailed arguments; but one brief example may suffice to indicate the usefulness of his impressive and detailed analysis of *The Seasons.* The opening lines of *Spring* are:

> COME, gentle Spring, ethereal mildness, come;
> And from the bosom of yon dropping cloud,
> While music wakes around, veiled in a shower
> Of shadowing roses, on our plains descend.

Cohen shows convincingly how "The image of birth, love and nourishment—of '*Spring*' descending from the bosom of the cloud followed by the renewal of nature and man—is the central image of the season" and that Thomson uses "The organizational procedure of recurring to the induction to *Spring,* amplifying and applying it, . . . [giving] this season a coherent development."[37] Thomson of course intended *The Seasons* to have the "thematic unity" suggested in the opening lines of *A Hymn On The Seasons,* appended to the first collected edition in 1730:

> THESE, as they change, Almighty Father! these
> Are but the varied God. The rolling year
> Is full of thee. Forth in the pleasing Spring
> Thy beauty walks, thy tenderness and love.
> . . . .
> Then comes thy glory in the Summer-months,
> With light and heat refulgent. . . .
> . . . .
> Thy bounty shines in Autumn unconfined,
> And spreads a common feast for all that lives.
> In Winter awful thou! with clouds and storms
> Around thee thrown, tempest o'er tempest rolled,
> Majestic darkness!
>
> (ll. 1–4, 8–9, 14–18)

The cycle of the year and Thomson's concern to find in it emblems of divinity provide at least a large loose framework and a consistent rationale for the poem. And although the descriptions, panegyrics, elegies, narratives, and catalogs which make up the poem often seem fortuitously related, Thomson does make use of some loose structural, thematic, and imagistic patterns and repetitions which provide considerable continuity in the poem. In *Spring* Thomson follows a "chain of being" order, considering the impact of spring first on matter, then on vegetable and animal, and finally on man. In *Summer,* "the progress of the poem is a description of a Summer's day," beginning at dawn, continuing through forenoon, noon, afternoon, sunset, evening, and night. In the other seasons as well there are perceptible patterns of passing through one or more days from dawn to dusk. Reinforcing the larger structure of the cycle of the year, each seasonal poem, even *Summer* to a small extent, has a structure or at least some suggestions of moving through the season from beginning to end. For the collected edition of 1730, Thomson nicely dovetailed his poems so as to suggest the transition from one season to another.

Smaller or larger patterns of movement from the particular to the general, from "description" to "reflection," are also characteristic of *The Seasons.* The appended "Hymn," for example, is intended to be a generalization on all the particulars which have gone before. Frequently, and at their best, Thomson's generalizations or "climaxes" are emotional outbursts rather than logical conclusions; often they are prayers or eulogies to God or Britain or "Philosophy," which break out by the accumulated heat of an "exulting" observation of the particulars of the beautiful, the marvelous, or the awe-inspiring in nature. Thomson in *Spring* describes the process:

> By swift degrees the love of nature works,
> And warms the bosom; till at last, sublimed
> To rapture and enthusiastic heat,
> We feel the present Deity, and taste
> The joy of God to see a happy world!
>
> (ll. 899–903)

For example, the best parts of *Spring* are the two lengthy sections on flowers and birds; and both sections begin with description and end with exclamations of praise of the Creator. In the first, catalogs of flowers are used to show the bounty of spring, which is manifested in "Infinite numbers, delicacies, smells,/With hues on hues expression cannot paint,/The breath of Nature, and her endless bloom" (ll.

553–55). The growing emotional involvement of the observer with such beauty and profusion culminates in an enthusiastic hymn of praise:

> Hail, Source of Being! Universal Soul
> Of heaven and earth! Essential Presence, hail!
> To thee I bend the knee; to thee my thoughts
> Continual climb, who with a master-hand
> Hast the great whole into perfection touched.
>
> (ll. 556–60)

This technique of moving from observation of particulars to generalizations which are frequently prayers or eulogies is found throughout *The Seasons.*

Overlapping this pattern of development from particular to general in the poem is a pattern of counterpointing or contrasting the actual and the ideal. Far from being a poem which argues shallowly that "whatever is, is right," *The Seasons* is fraught with the tension between Thomson's desire to believe in the perfection of God's world and the nagging reminders that observable reality does not add up to any such perfect scheme. Hence there is in the poem a repetitive and at times tortured weighing of the imperfection, disharmony, and mystery of the finite world of the present—which shifts and moves constantly under the eye—against a wished-for perfection, harmony, and clarity, frequently sought for in an imagined ideal past or future. Among Thomson's generalizations in *The Seasons* are found statements which stress the essential "rightness" of the world. Near the end of *Winter* we find "And what your bounded view, which only saw/ A little part, deemed evil is no more" (ll. 1066–67); and in the *Hymn,* "From seeming evil still educing good,/ And better thence again, and better still,/ In infinite progression" (ll. 114–16). In *Winter,* Thomson also stressed the fitness of the "moral world":

> Then would we try to scan the moral world,
> Which, though to us it seems embroiled, moves on
> In higher order, fitted and impelled
> By wisdom's finest hand, and issuing all
> In general good.
>
> (ll. 583–87)

But statements like these are in a sense *non sequiturs;* certainly they are among the feeblest and least convincing of the "reflections" with which Thomson follows up his rich and varied descriptions of a world which includes disharmony, cruelty, vast destructive forces, "wayward passions," and "vain pursuits"; a world where the "unconquerable lightning," for inexplicable reasons, with one stroke leaves the pine tree a "sad shattered trunk," the cattle "blasted" and "lifeless," and the perfectly innocent Amelia "A blackened corse." The frequent recurrence of such vividly imagined scenes in *The Seasons* jars severely the persuasiveness of the equally frequent generalizations about "perfection" and "The full-adjusted harmony of things" (*Autumn,* l. 835).

Ralph Cohen has noted of Thomson's passages dealing with more unpleasant aspects of nature and man that "All such passages are bound to be followed, immediately or shortly, in Thomson's procedure, by appeals to or assertions of God's goodness or man's power as indicative of God's goodness."[38] Thus the vivid passage on the agonies of a tortured lover in *Spring* is followed by a section describing an ideal marriage. A vigorous passage in *Summer,* in which the "dread ocean" overwhelms a ship to the "wild amazement" of a sailor transfixed by horror, closes with a reference to this same ocean's being tamed by the genius of navigation to bring "unbounded commerce" to the world. Following the terrible drowning of the swain led astray by the will-o'-the-wisp in *Autumn,* it is suggested that "At other times" the same light might assist the traveler to see his way. In each instance, however, the hopeful or ideal ending pales in vigor and reality beside what comes before. Cohen notes of the *Spring* lovers that "the ideal relationship is composed of qualities isolated from rather than realized in nature" and that "This dream of ideal love . . . lacks the excitement, the emotion, the trials of the dream of the fervent lover who sinks and is overwhelmed by 'the boiling Eddy.'"[39] In passages where we find juxtaposed vividly imagined representations of reality with briefer and paler "whatever is, is right" conclusions, it is tempting to find a breakdown of consistency between "description" and "reflection." Cohen, who would deny the breakdown, nevertheless admits that "the *Hymn* in its praise leads the poet to transcend the world, to disregard the suffering that he has described and, in a sense, to minimize and then falsify the immediacy of pain. It is a transcendent state, one indeed that becomes him more in the future world to which he finally turns than in one in which he lives."[40] Some degree of such minimizing and falsifying is characteristic not only of the *Hymn* but of Thomson's generalizations throughout *The Seasons.* Thomson's imaginative and emotional perceptions are considerably more convincing than the "philosophy" which he to some extent imposed on the poem. As pointed out earlier, his best "reflections" are emotional rather than "philosophical" or logical. Cohen finds the "unifying vision" in *The Seasons* to be "that God's love and wisdom, only fragmentarily perceptible in the beautiful and dangerous aspects of man and nature, will become fully perceptible in a future world."[41] There is no denying that the poem does include some such statement, and Cohen contributes to our understanding by reminding us of it. But whether this "unifying vision" satisfactorily accounts, either artistically or intellectually, for the breakdown of consistency between vivid and forceful portrayals of evil and the paler generalizations affirming "The full-adjusted harmony of things" (*Autumn,* l. 835) remains uncertain. The sheer weight and conviction of Thomson's portrayal of "all the tumult of a guilty world" (*Spring,* l. 939) tend to overwhelm his hopeful assertions "that God's love and wisdom . . . will become fully perceptible in a future world." This may be a "unifying vision," but visions after all are less realizable or convincing than vividly perceived and described reality.

To present the "ideal" side of things, Thomson resorts in *The Seasons* to what I will call a pattern of "retreats" from the "jarring world," which shifts and moves so constantly and which presents so many apparently inharmonious aspects. In *Summer* the "I" or observer of the poem retreats to the depths of a grove where, in "airy vision," he converses with "angels and immortal forms," who assure him of the "holy calm" and "harmony of mind" which will succeed this "stormy life." In *Winter,* he "retreats" to "A rural, sheltered, solitary scene" (l. 429) to converse in imagination with "sacred shades" of sages of the past; here, in perfect shelter, he and some "friends of pliant soul" pursue their philosophizing and decide that nature represents "full perfection" and that the "moral world . . . moves on . . . fitted and impelled/By wisdom's finest hand, and issuing all/In general good" (ll. 583–87). Frequently, the ideal world of calmness and benevolence is found in the retreat of a gentleman's country estate, such as Dodington's estate at Eastbury, Cobham's Stowe, or Lyttelton's Hagley Park, where "all the tumult of a guilty world" is shut out. Near the end of *Autumn,* a long idealized portrait of the rural life is represented as a kind of "golden age" existence, a life "which those who fret in guilt/And guilty cities never knew—the life/Led by primeval ages uncorrupt/When angels dwelt, and God himself, with man!" (ll. 1348–51). As a part of this pattern of "retreats" into the imagined ideal, it was probably inevitable that Thomson should include a long description of a "golden age" in the past, when nature and man were perfectly harmonious. Critics have devoted much attention to this passage (*Spring,* ll. 234–71) but have too infrequently mentioned that Thomson himself called it a "gaudy fable." To see the passage as a serious affirmation by Thomson that such an age, from which nature and men have since fallen away, once existed, is a misinterpretation. The passage, again rather feeble and conventional when compared to Thomson's descriptions of reality, is another example of a "retreat" to the ideal in the face of a bewildering reality. In fact, most of *Spring* might be said to represent one of the "retreats" of the poem; for the emphasis throughout is on a somewhat idealized harmony and sweetness where only the "smiling God" is seen. At the end of *The Seasons*, time is described as "wintry" and eternity imagined as "one unbounded Spring."

The speaker or "I" of the poem, faced with the bewildering mixture of harmony and disharmony in nature and man, hence retreats to shelter or into his imagination to express his faith that all is "By boundless love and perfect wisdom formed." Above all a seeker for knowledge and understanding, he chafes at man's present "bounded view" and throughout the poem ascends "heights," "summits," or "eminences" to observe and describe much larger landscapes or "prospects." This pattern of "prospects" has led to a great deal of emphasis on Thomson as a "landscape poet," supposedly influenced by Italian painters such as Claude Lorrain and Salvator Rosa. These "prospects" represent also, however, the poet's attempt to see larger patterns in nature and hence increase his understanding. Thomson imagined a future state to be one in which the "perfect whole" will be revealed "as the prospect wider spreads" (*Winter,* ll. 1047–48); and he prays excitedly to be allowed the highest "prospect," that from which all can be seen and understood:

> O Nature! all-sufficient! over all
> Enrich me with the knowledge of thy works;
> Snatch me to heaven; thy rolling wonders there,
> World beyond world, in infinite extent
> Profusely scattered o'er the blue immense,
> Show me; their motions, periods, and their laws
> Give me to scan.
>
> (*Autumn,* ll. 1352–58)

Although man's ability in his present state to "soar above this little scene of things" (*Autumn*, l. 966) is limited, his nature, as Shaftesbury said, is to make whatever "venturous and bold approach" he can "to know and contemplate [God]."[42] Hence the *Seasons* poet makes whatever attempt he can to increase the range of his "prospects"; he observes, catalogs, seeks scientific explanations, includes as much of the whole earth in his representation as possible, and climbs heights in an attempt to perceive larger and broader patterns. Even from these lookout points, however, the view is bounded; for, no matter how vast the prospect, the eye soon loses itself in the smoky (*Summer*, l. 1441) or dusky (*Spring*, l. 962) horizon. In addition to such patterns as those of "retreats" and "prospects," *The Seasons* is also characterized by the recurrence of a few basic and heavily emphasized aspects of the natural world, particularly storms, birds, sunrises and sunsets, and the British landscape.

There is, then, at least some loose continuity in theme, tone, style, and even structural pattern in *The Seasons*; but it is difficult to specify any yardstick for success or failure of "structure" or "unity" in a poem like *The Seasons*. Some critics have found a lack of "plan" or "method" in *The Seasons* and denounced it as a fault; and some, anxious to defend the poet, have looked desperately for evidence to assert the presence of "order" which others could not see. The inevitable inconclusiveness of such evidence is pointed up by a cynical critic who recently remarked that "any reader with a good wit (or fancy, in the Hobbesian sense) can make order out of anything containing enough language to establish any kind of repetition."[43] Actually, the most basic and successful qualities of *The Seasons* are such that perhaps "unity" or "structure" in a traditional sense hardly apply at all. Thomson was neither telling a story, presenting a logically structured argument, nor setting forth a neatly summarized or generalized system. *The Seasons* at its best has a present tense quality about it, with the "I" or observer engaged in excitedly describing, exclaiming, and rhapsodizing. Some of Thomson's attempts to impose a plan have been described above, such as the "Chain of Being" order in *Spring*, or the passing from dawn to dusk in *Summer*. He even moved some passages to more appropriate contexts while revising. He sometimes begins verse paragraphs which open new subjects with connectives like "and," "but," "thus," "nor," "or," "then," at least implying a continuity with what precedes. But Thomson's procedure of including as many of the "infinite" and "endless" manifestations of nature as possible, and dropping or adding freely in revision as something else demanded more attention, does not allow for neat structuring and continuity of the whole. His usual procedure for introducing a new topic is simply to launch into it; and verse paragraphs beginning with "Lo," "Behold," or simply "Now" usually signal a shift to a completely different scene. Finally, *The Seasons* is fragmented because the "nature" it describes is fragmented, at least insofar as man in his present state can determine. Its "infinite" manifestations present a bewildering and constantly changing combination of benevolence and destruction, kindness and cruelty, harmony and the chaotic. Furthermore, the sudden shifts of subject matter and style in *The Seasons* are suited not only to the elusive shifts of nature herself, but also to changes in the stance or mood of the observer. The progress of the poem is determined in part by such considerations as "What next catches his eye?" "What mood is he in?" A progress determined at least in part by what meets the "raptured eye,/Exulting swift" (*Summer*, ll. 1409–10) as it "sweeps" the "boundless landscape" does not lend itself to neat ordering or structuring. The "mood" of the "persona" determines at least in part whether nature is described in terms which are, in turn, "sublime," pathetic, exuberant, despairing, idealistic, scientific, or even mock-heroic. Also, as Ralph Cohen has pointed out, even the more "objective" representations in *The Seasons* are frequently "distancings" of the author's private feelings.

IX *Style*

From the late eighteenth century to the early twentieth century, critics of *The Seasons* regularly praised Thomson's descriptive powers and just as regularly flogged him for his "style" and "diction." As his position in literary history gradually came to be seen as that of a pioneer in bringing nature back to poetry, as an anomaly and a glimmer of dawning "romanticism" at odds with his own unimaginative, prosaic contemporaries, Thomson's clinging to "poetic diction," personification, a rhetorical style, and other rejected characteristics of eighteenth-century verse was seen as highly reprehensible. Wordsworth called his style "vicious";[44] Hazlitt labeled his art "gross, gaudy, and meretricious";[45] and a critic writing in 1877 roundly condemned Thomson's style as "heavy, cumbrous, oratorical, overloaded with epithets, full of artificial invocations, 'personified abstractions,' and insipid classicalities."[46] Such an interpretation is the inevitable result of the primary assumption that Thomson was a kind of anointed preparer of the way for Wordsworth. Given such an assumption, he then had to be condemned as unworthy because he did not have the proper Wordsworthian attitudes toward nature, poetry, tradition, and the use of language. Twentieth-century readers, still trained largely in methods and habits of nineteenth-century poetic traditions, probably will continue to find *The Seasons*, if they bother to read the poem at all, somewhat "artificial" and "pompous" in style, with its rhetorical, expansive, and Latinate qualities. But if we cannot fully appreciate or admire Thomson's diction, it is at least essential to attempt to understand it in some other terms than that the content (enlightened) and the style (utterly unenlightened) are completely at odds. Thomson's purposes and gifts were not what the nineteenth century assumed them to be; and that the "garment" of *The Seasons* was frequently quite well suited to Thomson's (not the nineteenth century's) conception of appropriate poetic response to nature has been amply demonstrated by Ralph Cohen's analysis in *The Unfolding of The Seasons* (1970).

In the preface (1726) to the second edition of *Winter*, Thomson identified himself with the "power of imagination," "exalting force of thought," and "affecting touch of sentiment" of the "sublime" tradition of poetry that "charmed the listening world from Moses down to Milton." He also praised the Book of Job, "crowned with a description of the grand works of Nature" and Virgil's *Georgics*, whose author's "devotion to the works of Nature" has been "the rapture of ages." He had also absorbed the highly emotional and devotional attitudes toward nature which were being fostered by the physico-theologians, the Newtonian scientists, and the Shaftesburian "enthusiasts." Nature is the grandest and most exalted of themes; therefore his adoption of the "grand style" was, to him if not to us, appropriate to such an "epic" theme. Miltonic blank verse was the obvious choice for a "heroic" measure; and he used many phrases and devices suggested by Milton and also by Virgil and other Latin poets. His expression is thus more rhetorical and effusive than we have been conditioned to expect of a "descriptive" poet. We have also lost the knowledge of, and taste for, the heavily Latinate terminology and sentence structure which Thomson and his contemporaries, with their assumption that English was "miserably inferior to Latin,"[47] inevitably imposed upon their expression. That Thomson's Latinisms, rhetorical tendencies, and "literary" language are not, as has been said, merely awkward results of straining for "Miltonic effects" has been convincingly demonstrated by D. Nichol Smith, who believes that "The style came easily to Thomson; it was natural to him." Thomson was a Scot; and the rhetoric, the large Latin element, and the "literary" English were all affected by his nationality and education. According to Smith, "The Scottish student has always been prone to rhetoric, and his tastes have been judiciously encouraged. . . . To the present day the Scottish student dearly loves a well-rounded resounding sentence." Smith also points out that "We are apt to forget the large place occupied by Latin in vernacular Scots. Latin was at one time as familiar to the educated Scot as his mother-tongue."[48] Of this facility in Latin and sometimes corresponding lack of ease in English expression, which leads to accusations of a "vicious" style, another critic has remarked, "To the educated Scot of the early and mid-century, who used the [Scottish] dialect in all his familiar relationships, who lectured in and listened to Latin on formal occasions, English was not even a second but actually a third language. It was deliberately learned, chiefly by study of the *Tatler,* the *Spectator* and the *Guardian.*"[49] Thomson's English style always retained something of the formal and rhetorical quality of a "classical" language learned from written models.

The common devices and mannerisms of Thomson's "diction" have roused critics to both censure and praise. R. D. Havens wrote in 1922 that "Calling things by their right names and speaking simply, directly, and naturally, . . . seems to have been his abhorrence."[50] But a later critic has constructed a very elaborate defense of Thomson's language and syntax as inventive, experimental, and appropriate: "In *The Seasons* Thomson undertook a series of experiments that led him to new uses of imagery, to trials in word combinations, to incorporation of scientific with classical and Biblical language in order to express his poetic vision of the world. The traditions of word order, sentence structure, diction and subject that he inherited he sought to use for his own new purposes."[51] Probably a more sensible interpretation would lie between these two extremes. If Thomson had considerably more justification for his peculiar diction than older critics have given him credit for, he nevertheless wrote at least some passages which are heavy going for today's readers, who will probably never recapture a respect either for his traditional devices or for some of his innovations.

In his effort to capture with language the complexities of his vision of the world, Thomson frequently interchanged parts of speech. He used adjectives for nouns ("blue immense," "blue serene"), adjectives for verbs ("serene his soul," "russets the plain"), nouns for verbs ("tempest the loosened brine"), verbs for nouns ("one wide waft"), transitive for intransitive verbs ("flame discloses wide"), or vice versa ("gazing the inverted landscape").[52] To cope with the "infinite" or "endless" variety of appearances nature presents, he habitually made up compounds, used usually in modifying positions. Most of these are participial ("seldom-meeting," "forest-rustling," "wide-shading," "deep-tinged," "various blossomed," "fierce-conflicting"); but he also used compounds like "richly-gorgeous" (adverb plus adjective), "gay-twinkle" (adjective used as adverb plus verb), "plume-dark" (noun plus adjective), or "labourer-ox" (noun plus noun).[53] Words of Latin derivation likely to be unfamiliar to the modern reader are frequent in *The Seasons:* "the vernant earth," "clamant children," "sap, detruded to the root," "lambs . . . convolved in friskful glee," the "wretch, exanimate by love," "the relucent stream," "a bursting stream auriferous plays," "the sun concoctive," and "relumed the soul." At times these words are even used with original Latin meanings they have lost in English, such as "the liberal [abundant] air" or "unessential [without substance] gloom."[54] We tend to dislike this, but Thomson's contemporaries knew and appreciated Latin; and he was actually trying to be both exact in description and economical in language with such words as "exanimate" and "relucent." Neither could be replaced by a single simpler word which retains the meaning. The "wretch, exanimate by love" would translate only to the "wretch, deprived of life or spirit by love"; and "the relucent stream" would translate to "the stream reflecting light" and would still not convey the connotation of "shining" which "relucent" also conveys. We are likely today to misinterpret such constructions as attempts to avoid simplicity and specific detail whereas the exact opposite is true. And, despite Thomson's reputation for wordiness and expansiveness, the interchangings of parts of speech and use of compound modifiers, if analyzed, can also be seen as language condensed rather than expanded. The "blue immense" means the "immense blue sky"; and "tempest the loosened brine" means "[a school of whales] churn up into a tempest the loosened brine." Far longer constructions would be required to convey in other words what is suggested by "plume-dark air" or "forest-rustling mountain."

Many critics have been particularly insulted by Thomson's use of that kind of circumlocution or periphrasis which calls birds "the plumy race" and fish "the finny tribe." Thomson uses a great many of these, calling fish the "finny race," or "glittering finny swarms," hibernating animals "furry nations," reindeer "the docile tribe," and birds "gay troops," "tuneful nations," "the glossy kind," "soft tribes," or "soaring race."[55] This has frequently been seen as the worst kind of "poetic diction," an artificial and false attempt to elevate and decorate the expression, a refusal to look at and describe nature in a natural and direct way. But, again, probably Thomson was using such phrases for precise functions rather than simply as a mindless, decorative use of traditional formulas. Geoffrey Tillotson and Ralph Cohen, among others, have come strongly to Thomson's defense in this regard. He by no means uses these circumlocutions as prevalently as some critics have given the impression he does; when he does, he has some specific function in mind, even if sometimes it is a function we no longer appreciate or even understand. References to birds as "tuneful nations" and "coy quiristers" are followed not only by references to thrush, wood-lark, blackbird, bullfinch, linnet, jay, rook, and dove, but also to the quality of the song of each and the sounds they make in harmony. Birds are referred to as "the glossy kind" in a section describing mating rituals, in which "glossy" plumage plays a primary attention-getting part. They are called "soft tribes" in a passage emphasizing their weakness and vulnerability to man's cruelty. They become "the soaring race" when Thomson describes the young birds' exhilaration in full flight for the first time. This is anything but a mindless and indiscriminate use of "poetic diction." The persistent use of terms like "tribe," "kind," "race," "breed," and "nation" was a traditional way of referring to the existence of distinct levels or groups in the hierarchy of the great Chain of Being. Such expressions as "finny race," "scaly breed," "feathered race," or "winged tribes" were not just "poetic diction" but accepted scientific nomenclature in Thomson's day, calling attention not only to separate levels of the great Chain but also to their particular adaptation to life at that level.[56] "Finny race" or "feathered race" identify groups of beings in the creation which are distinguished from others by fins or feathers. "Watery breed" or "airy race" would represent a slightly different sort of traditional classification. Geoffrey Tillotson reminds us that the term "heavenly bodies" is the lone survivor of this mode of scientific classification in our own day.[57] Hence it is difficult for us to accept these terms as the precise classifications which Thomson intended them to be. But when he says, "Batavian fleets/Defraud us of the glittering finny swarms/That heave our friths and crowd upon our shores" (*Autumn,* ll. 921–23), he means to convey something both more specific and more significant than if he had said "fish."

Such stylistic peculiarities as Thomson's circumlocutions and compound constructions have been emphasized all out of proportion to their importance, partly because of their obviousness and partly because of the hostility of so many critics to their use. The following passage can be used to illustrate Thomson's more characteristic style:

> Till, in the western sky, the downward sun
> Looks out effulgent from amid the flush
> Of broken clouds, gay-shifting to his beam.
> The rapid radiance instantaneous strikes
> The illumined mountain, through the forest streams,
> Shakes on the floods, and in a yellow mist,
> Far smoking o'er the interminable plain,
> In twinkling myriads lights the dewy gems.
> Moist, bright, and green, the landscape laughs around.
> Full swell the woods; their every music wakes,
> Mixed in wild concert, with the warbling brooks
> Increased, the distant bleatings of the hills,
> The hollow lows responsive from the vales,
> Whence, blending all, the sweetened zephyr springs.
> Meantime, refracted from yon eastern cloud,
> Bestriding earth, the grand ethereal bow
> Shoots up immense; and every hue unfolds,
> In fair proportion running from the red
> To where the violet fades into the sky.
> Here, awful Newton, the dissolving clouds
> Form, fronting on the sun, thy showery prism;
> And to the sage-instructed eye unfold
> The various twine of light, by thee disclosed
> From the white mingling maze.
>
> (*Spring*, ll. 189–212)

In this passage of 167 words in twenty-four lines, the most notable stylistic feature is the prevalence of modifying elements over clausal constructions. Using just enough finite verbs to keep some semblance of syntax, Thomson proceeds mainly by moving from one modified substantive to another, relying on adjectives, participles, adverbs, and prepositional phrases to convey the elaborate texture, diverse images, and constant motion characteristic of his word pictures. There are in this passage forty nouns, only fourteen verbs, and eighty modifying words, with twenty-three prepositional phrases also used as modifiers. The grandeur, light, color, and motion of the scene described is conveyed primarily by the twenty-four adjectives and especially by eighteen participles: "broken," "gay-shifting," "illumined," "smoking," "twinkling," "mixed," "warbling," "increased," "blending," "sweetened," "refracted," "bestriding," "running," "dissolving," "fronting," "sage-instructed," "disclosed," and "mingling." Thomson's sentence structure is of the "phrasal type" which Josephine Miles has found to be so prominent in eighteenth-century poetry: "The . . . phrasal type employs an abundance of adjectives and nouns, in heavy modifications and compounding of subjects, in a variety of phrasal constructions, including verbs turned to participles; it is a cumulative way of speaking." Blank verse is appropriate to such an expression, which is likely to have a "line-by-line progression, and cumulative participial modification in description and invocation without stress on external rhyming or grouping." Professor Miles finds the cumulative phrasal sentence structure and corresponding lack of finite verbs and clausal subordinations to be highly characteristic of the "sublime" poem of the eighteenth century, of which *The Seasons* is one of the best examples.[58]

A frequent, almost standard critical contention has been that Thomson's blank verse "is a blank verse which has been passed through the strainer of the heroic couplet."[59] Reference has been made to his use of "lines of the same marked cadence," lack of stress inversions, infrequent "run-over" lines, and groups of "unrimed couplets." This contention has undoubtedly some validity, but it is an oversimplified and not very helpful guide. It is not a sufficient generalization to say that Thomson's habitual unit of expression is "two or three lines that fall into unrimed couplets or triplets."[60] Critics have assumed that Thomson was attempting to write Miltonic "metrical paragraphs" and that he fell short in using "run-over" lines to achieve Miltonic blank verse effects. He had, they say, too much of the couplet habit "in his blood" to make masterful use of Milton's complicated instrument. But Thomson was neither in bondage to the couplet, to the metrical paragraph, or to some imagined bastard combination of the two. Johnson realized this and said of Thomson that "His blank verse is no more the blank verse of Milton or of any other poet than the rhymes of Prior are the rhymes of Cowley. His numbers, his pauses, his diction, are of his own growth."[61] Thomson's "unit" of expression is usually the single line, with larger "cumulations" of lines which have less to do with syntax than with sounds and images. To assume that Thomson was always trying to write like

Milton is as absurd, and as common, as the assumption that he ought to have been writing like Wordsworth. The following statement by R. D. Havens makes no sense unless you assume that Thomson was simply trying ineptly to write Miltonic blank verse: "The truth seems to be that when off his guard Thomson relapsed into writing not metrical paragraphs but separate lines, and that he had to exert himself to vary his pauses and to avoid a slight break after every tenth syllable."[62] In the passage from *The Seasons* quoted above, the sentences range in length from one line to five lines. The syntax of sentences consisting mostly of nouns, connectives, and modifiers cannot be maintained through many lines and sometimes gets lost in even a short sentence. Probably the length to which Thomson carried sentences in his blank verse does not matter much. F. W. Bateson has accurately said of *The Seasons* that its progression is "not repetitive . . . or organic . . . or logical, . . . but cumulative." It is the "sheer juxtaposition of images" rather than the sometimes careless syntactical connections that is most basic. Furthermore, the "hurry" and "confusion" of images, which sometimes leaves syntax behind, enhances the "sublime" quality of a poem like *The Seasons*.[63]

Finally, the "style" of *The Seasons* is not uniform, but is varied to match the different subjects and moods of the poem. Thomson could write in the "grand style" in his "sublime" descriptions, prayers, or patriotic effusions. But for gentler scenes and softer moods he is capable of more restrained lines, as in much of *Spring* or in such lines as these from *Autumn:*

> As in the hollow breast of Apennine,
> Beneath the shelter of encircling hills,
> A myrtle rises, far from human eye,
> And breathes its balmy fragrance. . . .
>
> (ll. 209–12)

Among other modes of expression Thomson incorporates into *The Seasons* is the mock-herioc:

> Perhaps some doctor of tremendous paunch,
> Awful and deep, a black abyss of drink,
> Outlives them all; and, from his buried flock
> Retiring, full of rumination sad,
> Laments the weakness of these latter times.
>
> (*Autumn,* ll. 565–69)

At times Thomson will indicate which "style" he is attempting, as when he remarks early in *Winter* that his Muse will try "to soar,/To swell her note with all the rushing winds,/To suit her sounding cadence to the floods;/As is her theme, her numbers wildly great" (ll. 24–27). At the beginning of the section on the music of birds in *Spring*, he says, "Lend me your song, ye nightingales! oh, pour/The mazy-running soul of melody/Into my varied verse!" (ll. 576–78). In the passage which follows, careful attention is paid to sound effects, as in "their modulations mix/Mellifluous" and ". . . the stock-dove breathes/A melancholy murmur through the whole" (ll. 609–10, 612–13). In *Summer*, Thomson delivers his catalog of tributes to Britain's "sons of glory" in exalted tones: "Alfred thine,/In whom the splendour of heroic war,/And more heroic peace . . . / . . . the best of kings!" (ll. 1479–83). But he changes his instrument when he comes to Britannia's daughters: "May my song soften as thy daughters I,/Britannia, hail!" (ll. 1580–81). The lines which follow avoid boldness and harshness of diction and rhythm. Furthermore, Thomson had a good ear and usually succeeded in adapting his sounds and rhythms to his subject matter.

X *Revisions*

Between 1726 and 1746, the poems which make up *The Seasons* were greatly expanded and substantially revised. *Winter* (first published in 1726) exists in six separate versions, *Summer* (first published in 1727) in four versions, *Spring* (first published in 1728) in four versions, *Autumn* (first published in 1730) in three versions, and the *Hymn* (first published in 1730) in three versions. This process of adding and revising began early in the history of *The Seasons*, when Thomson published a second edition of *Winter* in June, 1726, expanded by 58 lines from the 405 line first edition of three months earlier. The first collected *Seasons*, a quarto subscription volume of 1730, which included *Autumn* and the *Hymn* for the first time, contained altered and expanded versions of *Spring, Summer,* and *Winter.* Another major rewriting was undertaken for the edition of 1744, and the final edition of Thomson's lifetime in 1746 was also slightly revised. In the course of revision, *Winter* and *Summer* underwent greater changes than the other poems, partly because the later poems, *Spring, Autumn,* and the *Hymn*, were written when Thomson had more fully in mind his plan for a larger poem on the full course of the seasons and thus had less need to change them subsequently. Also, winter and summer are the seasons of extremes in nature and offer greater possibilities for the addition of the "sublime" scenes which make up a large part of the later additions to *The Seasons*.

The complex revisions of *The Seasons* have always been a major stumbling block for critics and interpreters of Thomson's art. Even to chart completely all the revisions was considered by most nineteenth-century Thomson scholars too impossibly difficult to attempt, and consequently statements made about the revisions were for a long time extremely haphazard. Not until 1908 were variorum editions made available by Otto Zippel and J. Logie Robertson. But twentieth-century critics have become increasingly aware that ". . . it is only by careful analysis of the revisions that one can finally understand Thomson's overall intentions in the poem."[64] The excellent full-length studies of *The Seasons* by A. D. McKillop (1942), Patricia Spacks (1959), and Ralph Cohen (1964, 1970) show full cognizance of the importance of the revisions in interpreting *The Seasons*. The scope and difficulty of the problem is such, however, that a book devoted entirely to a full analysis of the revisions, perhaps a companion volume to Zippel's variorum edition, would be a welcome addition to Thomson studies. Difficult even for the Thomson specialist, the revisions are an even greater problem to other scholars. A recent scholar, for example, attributes to the influence of George Lyttelton's "prudery" the change in *Winter* (l. 1037) from "nights of secret guilt" to "gay-spent festive nights."[65] A glance at the 1730 edition will show that this alteration was made several years before Thomson was associated with Lyttelton. Another scholar has attempted to demonstrate that Thomson and Pope were friends in 1727 when *Summer* was published by citing a passage (ll. 1425–28) which was in fact not added to *The Seasons* until 1744.[66] Such slips are far from unique and demonstrate the need for caution in making statements about *The Seasons* without checking carefully the revisions.

Despite the significance of the revisions to full scholarly understanding of Thomson's aims and artistry in *The Seasons*, most readers will perhaps be content with only the final version of the poem. Thomson intended his last effort to be the one we would read, and readers in the heyday of his popularity were seemingly unhampered in their love and appreciation of *The Seasons* by the lack of variorum apparatus in the hundreds of thousands of copies they bought and cherished. In any event, a brief introductory book on

Thomson can only sketch in its broadest outlines the process and result of revisions in *The Seasons.*

The most noticeable result of the revisions is a substantial increase in length. Thomson's poem is about "nature," with loosely associated scenes and themes of natural description; human benevolence; social and political concerns; scientific, philosophical, and theological speculation; and autobiographical concerns. As such it was infinitely expandable; and Thomson in his revisions was always on the lookout to expand it. While it would be foolish and unfair to deny that Thomson was in pursuit of artistic purposes in expanding *The Seasons*, it is nevertheless true that he was struggling to make a living by his pen and only realistic to point out that "To earn money from every succeeding edition of *The Seasons*, Thomson had to make it bigger and better than its predecessors, to incorporate more and more new material that might attract purchasers."[67] This was true both in the late 1720s, when he was with difficulty promoting subscriptions for a "collected" edition of *The Seasons*, and in the early 1740s, when he was desperately trying to get together enough money to marry Elizabeth Young. *The Seasons* grew under his pen from the 405 lines of the original *Winter* to 4470 lines in 1730 and to 5541 lines by 1746. The amount of new material in later versions is even greater than these figures indicate, since substantial passages from earlier versions were also dropped along the way. The first version of *Winter* in March, 1726, is mostly a "nature" poem written from the poet's own experience and is not much concerned with many of the loosely associated themes later introduced into *The Seasons*, such as science, rationalistic physico-theology, politics, or humanitarianism. Yet the original plan was never entirely submerged in the later *Seasons*, as is sometimes said to be the case. Descriptive passages followed by moral or religious sentiments; the sublimity of nature; the notion that nature can awaken feelings of benevolence in man: all these are basic to the first *Winter* and remain basic to *The Seasons* in its final form.

The expansion of *The Seasons* was achieved partly by simply adding more scenes considered appropriate to a particular season. Hence Thomson added to *Spring* a section on fishing (ll. 379–466), added to *Summer* sections on haymaking and sheepshearing (ll. 352–431), and greatly expanded the descriptions of natural scenes in *Winter*, including descriptions of both village (ll. 617–29) and city (ll. 630–55) life. Very substantial expansions of *Summer* and *Winter* were accomplished by adapting from travel and geography books descriptions of the torrid and polar zones of the world, in order to develop further the "sublime" qualities of these seasons of climatic extremes. Thomson also introduced into later editions compliments to friends and patrons, such as George Lyttelton (*Spring*, ll. 904–62); William Pitt and Lord Cobham (*Autumn*, ll. 1037–81); Lord Chesterfield (*Winter*, ll. 656–90); Elizabeth Young (*Spring*, ll. 483–88; *Summer*, ll. 1401 ff.); Elizabeth Stanley (*Summer*, ll. 564–84); Alexander Pope (*Summer*, ll. 1427–28; *Winter*, ll. 550–54); and James Hammond (*Winter*, ll. 555–71). Most of these latter additions have political as well as personal implications, since Lyttelton, Cobham, Pitt, and Chesterfield were leaders in the Opposition to Walpole; and both Pope and Hammond were, like Thomson, poets prominent in the service of the Opposition. This procedure of adding compliments to political allies could be reversed, as when Thomson dropped from *Autumn* in 1744 an earlier compliment to the royal family. Thomson attempted to mesh these tributes into the larger plan and pattern of *The Seasons*. Lyttelton is introduced into *Spring* as an example of the benevolent man, moved by the serenity and beauty of nature at his country estate Hagley Park to contemplate "with warm benevolence of mind" the good of his countrymen. The ghost of Elizabeth Stanley is introduced as one of the "sacred band" of spirits who visit the poet in one of his ecstatic visions. Pope and Hammond are introduced into a catalog of Greek, Roman, and British sages already present in *Winter*.

Between 1726 and 1730, Thomson absorbed into his plan for *The Seasons* large doses of science, humanitarianism, matter from travel books, and unorthodox theology. In 1730, he gave his readers some science lessons, such as these lines in *Winter:*

> What art thou, frost? and whence are thy keen stores
> Derived, thou secret all-invading power,
> Whom even the illusive fluid cannot fly?
> Is not thy potent energy, unseen,
> Myriads of little salts, or hooked, or shaped
> Like double wedges, and diffused immense
> Through water, earth, and ether?
>
> (ll. 714–20)

or the section in *Autumn* where he elaborates on a theory of how water gets back uphill, losing salt as it soaks upward through the "sandy stratum," a section which he expanded further in 1744 by adding scientific arguments against the theory (ll. 736–72). By 1730, the increased social and humanitarian content of *The Seasons* could be expected to arouse more tender and benevolent feelings in its readers, as when Thomson praised the work of a committee looking into wretched prison conditions:

> And here can I forget the generous band
> Who, touched with human woe, redressive searched
> Into the horrors of the gloomy jail?
> Unpitied and unheard where misery moans,
> Where sickness pines, where thirst and hunger burn,
> And poor misfortune feels the lash of vice;
>
> (*Winter*, ll. 359–64)

or as he described the farmer frozen to death in the snow and exclaimed, "Alas!/Nor wife nor children more shall he behold,/Nor friends, nor sacred home" (*Winter*, ll. 315–17). Also, that Thomson by 1730 had drifted from his boyhood Presbyterianism toward the more fashionable rationalistic theologies of the day can be seen in the addition of lines like these:

> Hence larger prospects of the beauteous whole
> Would gradual open on our opening minds;
> And each diffusive harmony unite
> In full perfection to the astonished eye.
> Then would we try to scan the moral world,
> Which, though to us it seems embroiled, moves on
> In higher order, fitted and impelled
> By wisdom's finest hand, and issuing all
> In general good.
>
> (*Winter*, ll. 579–87)

Regardless of the later extensive additions and revisions, Thomson had by 1730 arrived at his "plan" for *The Seasons*; the concluding *Hymn*, intended to be a kind of summary statement of the overall system of nature described in the poem, was not later altered substantially. As A. D. McKillop has said, "Thomson's fundamental views in religion and philosophy were fully formed by 1730 and . . . the extensive later additions were of a more specific character, elaborating themes already present in the early redactions and deriving their content largely, though by no means exclusively, from the literature of science and travel."[68] Thomson continued to expand *The Seasons* by such devices as gradually increasing the length of catalogs of Greek, Roman, and British "sages" in *Winter* and of English worthies in *Summer.* The 1744 *Seasons* also has more political and patriotic overtones, perhaps as a natural aftermath of Thomson's heavy political involvement and the writing of *Liberty* in the 1730s. The introduction of tributes to his political friends of the Opposition party has already been mentioned. Other examples would be the jingoistic passage on Britain introduced into *Summer:*

> Wide glows her land: her dreadful thunder hence
> Rides o'er the waves sublime, and now, even now,
> Impending hangs o'er Gallia's humbled coast;
> Hence rules the circling deep, and awes the world.
> (ll. 428–31)

or the *Liberty*-like sentiments introduced into passages descriptive of inhabitants of the torrid zone, who lack the "softening arts of peace" and "government of laws" (*Summer,* ll. 875, 881). Other 1744 passages reminiscent of *Liberty* are the description of the northern hordes who had once invaded the "enfeebled south" and "relumed the flame/Of lost mankind in polished slavery sunk" (*Winter,* ll. 838–39) and a lengthy tribute to Peter the Great, of whom Thomson remarks, "What cannot active government perform,/New-moulding man?" (*Winter,* ll. 950–51).

If the sheer weight and diversity of the additions to *The Seasons* inevitably detracted from its compactness of form and unity of purpose, it is nevertheless true that the overall effect of the revisions represents improvement and conscious artistry. For as Thomson dropped, shifted, or altered passages, lines, and words, he reduced obscurity, awkwardness, and inconsistency and worked toward a greater consistency of tone and meaning within each season and within the larger whole. While adding "sublime" passages showing the great power and force of nature, he dropped long passages which he came to see were merely bizarre, sensational, or gaudy, such as "petrified city" in *Summer* and the more excessive passages of the "golden age" fable in *Spring.* He also shifted passages to other locations within the poem in order to achieve better continuity. In 1730, *Autumn* absorbed sections of earlier versions of *Winter* and *Summer* which are more appropriate and effective in their new context. A passage originally in *Spring,* detailing the marvelous variety of life as revealed by the microscope, was moved in 1744 to *Summer* (ll. 287–317), where it follows appropriately a section on "ten thousand different tribes" of insects and leads naturally into a passage on the limitations of man's awareness of all that is contained within "the mighty chain of beings." A long patriotic tribute to "Happy Britannia" in the early part of *Summer* was so obviously a digression that Thomson took six lines to explain why he had been "nobly digressive." In 1744, he placed this passage near the end of *Summer*, where it follows naturally a newly added "prospect" of the beauties of British landscape, which could be expected to inspire in the observer larger patriotic thoughts of "Happy Britannia."

Thomson's alterations of lines and words also frequently make sense in light of his total plan. A few examples must suffice, although this kind of change is very extensive in the revisions. In later editions of *Spring,* the "brown-browed hill" became the "withered hill" (l. 87) and the "influential sun" became the "world-reviving sun" (l. 51). Both changes reflect the consciousness in early spring of winter just past. Thomson made his "pictures" more vivid and accurate in later alterations. "The forest running round, the rising spire" became in 1744 "The forest darkening round, the glittering spire" (*Spring,* l. 524). Thomson was painfully conscious of the difficulty of capturing in words a natural scene of "Infinite numbers, delicacies, smells, / With hues on hues expression cannot paint" (*Spring,* ll. 553–54). Hence it is interesting to see him rewriting in 1744 a passage in *Spring,* attempting to get closer to his ambition to "paint like Nature." In 1730 this passage read,

> The daisy, primrose, violet darkly blue,
> Dew-bending cowslips, and of nameless dies
> Anemonies, auriculas a tribe
> Peculiar powder'd with a shining sand,
> Renunculas, and iris many-hued.

The passage as revised for the later editions shows Thomson capturing more of the "numbers, delicacies, smells" of nature:

> The daisy, primrose, violet darkly blue,
> And polyanthus of unnumbered dyes;
> The yellow wall-flower, stained with iron brown,
> And lavish stock, that scents the garden round:
> From the soft wing of vernal breezes shed,
> Anemones; auriculas, enriched
> With shining meal o'er all their velvet leaves;
> And full ranunculus, of glowing red.
>
> (ll. 531–38)

In his continuing attempt to give *Summer* a dominant quality of oppressive heat and light, he changed in later editions "yonder fields" to "brightening fields" (l. 1), ". . . the sun/Shoots through the expanding air a torrid gleam" to ". . . the sun/Darts on the head direct his forceful rays" (ll. 432–33), "Prevailing heat" to "All-conquering heat" (l. 451), and "Beam not so hard!" to "Beam not so fierce!" (l. 453). Also, the dominant quality of fierceness and destructiveness in *Winter* is further emphasized by changing the "red evening-sky" to the "grim evening-sky" (l. 14) and the "still rage of Winter" to the "fierce rage of Winter" (l. 722). References to winter in other parts of the poem are altered to the same effect. In *Autumn*, the "red north,/With winter charged" became the "bleak north,/With winter charged" (ll. 60–61); and in *Summer*, "Winter" became "Fierce Winter" (l. 345). Another aspect of the marvelous in nature which Thomson gradually became more aware of is its sheer unbounded spaciousness. In *Summer*, for example, "far as the darted eye/Can pierce" became in 1744 "far as the ranging eye/Can sweep" (ll. 434–35); "shoots the trembling glow" became "spreads the widening glow" (l. 49); and the "face of nature . . . all unveiled" became "wide unveiled" (l. 202). Also, the dropping of at least some of the more difficult Latinate terminology of *The Seasons* in revisions can only be considered an improvement, as, for example, when "attenuates to" was changed to "melts into," "mildly elucent" to "faint-gleaming," or "detruded" to "imprisoned."

That Thomson did improve the poetry of at least parts of *The Seasons* can be seen clearly in his taking some very commonplace lines from the story of Palemon and Lavinia and replacing them with a beautiful poetic image. In 1730, the lines read,

> Recluse among the woods; if city-dames
> Will deign their faith. And thus she went compell'd
> By strong necessity, with as serene,
> And pleas'd a look as patience can put on,
> To glean Palemon's fields.

In later editions, these lines are replaced by

> Recluse amid the close-embowering woods.
> As in the hollow breast of Apennine,
> Beneath the shelter of encircling hills,
> A myrtle rises, far from human eye,
> And breathes its balmy fragrance o'er the wild—
> So flourished blooming, and unseen by all,
> The sweet Lavinia; till at length, compelled
> By strong necessity's supreme command,
> With smiling patience in her looks she went
> To glean Palemon's fields.
>
> (*Autumn*, ll. 208–17)

XI A Poem Sacred to the Memory of Sir Isaac Newton

Sir Isaac Newton stirred the imagination of the eighteenth century far more than any other scientific figure. By the time of his death at the age of eighty-four on March 20, 1727, he had long been not only a universally known luminary of the scientific community but also the object of great public veneration. A layman's view of Newton's unique contribution to eighteenth-century science and physico-theology can be seen in Addison's *Spectator*, no. 543 (November 22, 1712): "The more extended our Reason is, and the more able to grapple with immense Objects, the greater still are those Discoveries which it makes of Wisdom and Providence in the Work of the Creation. A Sir *Isaac Newton,* who stands up as the Miracle of the present Age, can look through a whole Planetary system; consider it in its Weight, Number, and Measure; and draw from it as many Demonstrations of infinite Power and Wisdom, as a more confined Understanding is able to deduce from the System of an Human Body." Pope also summed up the feeling of the age toward Newton in his "Epitaph. Intended for Sir Isaac Newton," when he said "Nature, and Nature's Laws lay hid in Night./God said, *Let Newton be!* and All was *Light.*"[69]

Thomson's reverence for Newton was such that it is entirely natural that he should have postponed work on *Spring* in early 1727 to write his panegyric on the great scientist who had just died. Thomson's poem, published on May 8, 1727, and immediately popular, is not only an elegy and panegyric but also a compendium of some of the important ideas of both the *Principia* and the *Opticks.* Thomson's absorption of Newtonian science was begun during his college days in Edinburgh and continued after 1725 in England, particularly during his tenure in 1726 as a tutor at Watt's Academy in London, a center for the study and popularization of Newtonian philosophy. Thomson's period of residence at Watt's Academy in 1726 was also the main period of his work on *Summer* (published in February, 1727), which Marjorie Nicolson has appropriately called "the book of *The Seasons* in which Thomson's descriptions of light and of the sun are most frequent, and in which reminiscences of Newtonian theories most abound."[70] By the time Thomson wrote his poem on Newton, therefore, he not only admired Newton greatly, but had also made substantial and significant use of his knowledge of Newton's theories in *Summer.*

Thomson's poem on Newton might almost be considered a part of *The Seasons*; for it was not only written at the same time, but uses the same verse form, is concerned with identical themes, and shares the same "sublime" mode of expression. Thomson may well have thought of the poem as part and parcel with *Spring, Summer, Autumn, Winter,* and the *Hymn;* for he collected all six poems in 1730 under the title *The Seasons*. The poem eulogizes Newton as "Britain's Boast" and summarizes his achievements. Most importantly, "he by the blended Power/Of *Gravitation* and *Projection* saw/The whole in silent Harmony revolve" (ll. 40–42). As in *The Seasons*, Thomson moves from an itemization of the particulars of the Newtonian universe to a hymn of praise:

> O unprofuse Magnificence divine!
> O Wisdom truly perfect! thus to call
> From a few Causes such a Scheme of Things,
> Effects so various, beautiful, and great,
> An Universe compleat! And, O belov'd
> Of Heaven! whose well-purg'd penetrative Eye,
> The mystic Veil transpiercing, inly scan'd
> The rising, moving, wide-establish'd Frame!
>
> (ll. 68–75)

Another section of the poem consists of a lavish parade of the spectrum colors, first "untwisted" by Newton from "the whitening undistinguish'd Blaze." Thomson describes each color from red to violet, notes their "mingling" in the rainbow, and moves again to rhapsodic praise:

> Did ever Poet image aught so fair,
> Dreaming in whispering Groves, by the hoarse Brook!
> Or Prophet, to whose Rapture Heaven descends!
> Even now the setting Sun and shifting Clouds,
> Seen, *Greenwich,* from thy lovely Heights, declare
> How just, how beauteous the *Refractive Law.*
>
> (ll. 119–24)

The passage just quoted can be used to illustrate the same style and sentence structure noted in *The Seasons*. The expression shows the same tendency to elevation and exclamation and also the same reliance on nouns, adjectives, and participles to achieve desired effects. Only three finite verbs—"did image," "descends," and "declare"—are used in the passage.

As a frame for his tribute to Newton and a summary of his accomplishments, Thomson imagines him in a typically "Newtonian" heaven, not in blessed rest, but continuing to observe "new wonders." Marjorie Nicolson has said of the early eighteenth-century scientists that "they can conceive no life in the future more perfect than one in which they will continue to discover the wonders of Nature. Their Utopia is no heaven city of perpetual calm, but an Eternity in which they may expect through infinite time the delights of discovery, of accomplishment, of fuller and fuller (though never complete) contemplation of the beauties of Nature, and—one likes to believe—celestial 'Elaboratories' with perfect microscopes."[71] Newton would thus have been pleased that Thomson consigned him to a future life where he could continue, perhaps with improved mathematics and a larger telescope, "Comparing Things with Things, in Rapture lost" (l. 195).

CHAPTER 3

The "Nobler Way": Liberty *and the Tragedies*

JOSEPH Warton noted in 1756 that "It may be observed in general, that description of the external beauties of nature, is usually the first effort of a young genius, before he hath studied manners and passions."[1] In a similar vein, a reviewer of the early *Seasons* had lauded in 1728 Thomson's plan to produce a tragedy, which would be "Entertainment in a nobler way; when the Author shall rise from the *still Life* of Poetry, to represent the Passions of Mankind. . . ."[2] In late 1730, after the publication of the first complete *Seasons* and the production of *Sophonisba,* Thomson was "trembling" and "burning" with the thought that he might be capable of an "Epic performance." Thus the very substantial effort he exerted on the epiclike *Liberty* (1735–1736) and his five classical tragedies (1730–1748) represents a perfectly normal, if largely abortive, movement into "nobler" themes of morality and humanity and "higher" forms of the tragedy and epic. These later works represent, however, shifts of emphasis rather than complete departures from the concerns of *The Seasons.* The central themes of public virtue, benevolence, and patriotism in *Liberty* and the tragedies represent the full development of ideas which were present to some extent in the earliest versions of *The Seasons* and which were greatly expanded and emphasized in later revisions. Thomson added a passage to *Winter* in 1730, outlining a search for truth which progresses through nature, the "moral world," and history:

> Hence larger prospects of the beauteous whole
> Would gradual open on our opening minds;
> And each diffusive harmony unite,
> In full perfection, to th' astonish'd eye.
> Thence would we plunge into the moral world;
> Which, tho' more seemingly perplex'd, moves on
> In higher order; fitted, and impell'd,
> By Wisdom's finest hand, and issuing all
> In universal good. Historic truth
> Should next conduct us thro' the deeps of time:
> Point us how empire grew, revolv'd, and fell,
> . . . .
> As thus we talk'd,
> Our hearts would burn within us, would inhale
> That portion of divinity, that ray
> Of purest heaven, which lights the glorious flame
> Of patriots, and of heroes.[3]

From the beginning, *The Seasons* also included passages suggesting a close correspondence between a thoughtful, reverent observation of nature and virtue, benevolence, and patriotism. In the 1730 *Autumn,* for example, the lover of nature experiences "correspondent passions":

> As fast the correspondent passions rise,
> As varied, and as high: devotion rais'd
> To rapture, and divine astonishment.
> The love of Nature unconfin'd, and chief
> Of humankind; the large, ambitious wish,
> To make them blest.[4]

The unifying concept in Thomson's treatment of nature, morality, or social systems is "order" or "harmony." *The Seasons*, as previously discussed, is primarily a poem about order in nature. In an age when the proper study of mankind was man, and moral considerations were paramount, it was natural and logical for Thomson to focus his concern for order on the "moral world" as revealed in history's panorama of human greatness and degradation, the rise and fall of political systems, and the vacillating fortunes of culture and liberty.

A large proportion of this later body of work is "political," not only in the sense that the working out in history of the ideas Thomson was interested in is ultimately a history of politics but also in the sense that much of his writing concerns the fate of liberty and culture as he saw them encouraged or threatened by the politics of his own time. The final purpose of his work is didactic. Poetry and the other arts should be, as they had been in ancient Greece, handmaids to "public virtue";[5] and the theater should function as "the School which forms the Manners of the Age."[6] Thomson's delineations of the causes of the rise and decline of liberty in Greece and Rome and his depictions in drama of the triumphs and mistakes of noble leaders of the past are lessons for his contemporaries. It is not surprising that such severely didactic motives produced works which have been considered "artistic failures." The noble motives of Thomson's political writing were considerably diluted, however, by his increasing involvement in "party politics" and jingoistic flag waving for the glories of British maritime commerce. Thomson was only one of many eighteenth-century poets and dramatists who propagandized the glories of progress under Whig policy in poetry which has been called "Whig panegyric." Even more deadening was his increasing involvement in the 1730s with the opposition to Walpole. It would be unfair to Thomson to classify *Liberty* strictly as an "Opposition poem"; but by the later 1730s Thomson's involvement with Prince Frederick, Lyttelton, and other leaders of the Opposition party was leading him to write largely from the motive of attacking and degrading Walpole. His once promising talent and great ambitions sank in this period almost to the level of a party hack. Nevertheless, *Liberty,* the tragedies, and some lesser works with political content form a substantial part of Thomson's output. Despite the generally unfavorable verdict of posterity, these works are of great significance in his career as poet and playwright.

I Liberty *(1735–1736)*

Liberty is a long blank verse poem of 3,378 lines. It consists of five separately published parts: part 1—"Ancient and Modern Italy Compared"; part 2—"Greece"; part 3—"Rome"; part 4—"Britain"; and part 5—"The Prospect." The speaker throughout is the Goddess of Liberty, who appears to the poet, amid the ruins of Rome, and not only speaks to him but also creates for him a vision of the action which passes before his eyes as she speaks. In Thomson's dedication of the poem to Prince Frederick, he declared it to be an "attempt to trace Liberty from the first ages down to her excellent establishment in Great Britain."[7] Part 1 consists mainly of a description of the "dejected," "sordid," and "desponding" state of modern Italy under the presiding genius of "Oppression." A contrast is drawn between the present sad state of affairs and the glory and prosperity of ancient Rome. Britain is admonished to learn from this example what happens when a society is deprived of liberty. In part 2, the growth of liberty is traced briefly from the "dawn of time" down to its establishment in "unrivalled Greece!/My fairest reign! where every power benign/Conspired to blow the flower of human kind,/And lavished all that genius can inspire" (ll. 86–89). Sparta and Athens are described as two differing but equally strong bastions of liberty. Philosophy, oratory, poetry, music, sculpture, painting, and architecture are described as "unblemished handmaids" of "public virtue" in Greece (ll. 365–66). But Grecian liberty was eventually undermined by luxury and corruption:

> Unless corruption first deject the pride
> And guardian vigour of the free-born soul,
> All crude attempts of violence are vain;
> For, firm within, and while at heart untouched,
> Ne'er yet by force was freedom overcome.
> But, soon as Independence stoops the head,
> To vice enslaved and vice-created wants,
> Then to some foul corrupting hand, whose waste
> These heightened wants with fatal bounty feeds—
> From man to man the slackening ruin runs,
> Till the whole state unnerved in slavery sinks.
>
> (ll. 490–500)

In part 3, the spirit of liberty moves to the Greek colonies in Italy and then to Rome, where liberty achieves a peak in the republic, under which all private interest is subjected to the "common good." But, as in Greece, liberty is in time weakened by luxury: "The pestilence of mind, a fevered thirst/For the false joys which luxury prepares" (ll. 374–75). Luxury breeds corruption which in turn brings a deluge of despotism and ruin. Liberty, her place in Rome usurped, pursues her flight northward and westward, stirs up the northern Gothic hordes to vengeance on corrupt Rome, and leaves the earth entirely.

Part 4 opens with an account of the "Gothic darkness" of the Middle Ages, described as a time of chaos and disorder, presided over by the "tyrannic rule," "persecuting zeal," and "idiot Superstition" of the medieval church. At the Renaissance, Liberty returns to earth. She revisits Italy briefly and, although unable to rout political tyranny, does unearth both the artifacts and the spirit of ancient Greek sculpture, which fosters the growth of Renaissance art. Again taking flight northward and westward, Liberty fosters "small republics" and "free states and cities" here and there in Europe. Further north, she influences in her course the freedom-loving peoples of "vast Germania" and "wintry Scandinavia." Upon arrival in Britain, she joins forces with the goddess Britannia to begin a "permanent" reign, abetted by the native qualities of Courage, Benevolence, Justice, Sincerity, Reason, Retirement, Independence, Virtue, Labour, and Religion. At this point, Liberty recites a long history of England, tracing the gradual growth of freedom and suppression of tyranny from the Celtic beginnings down to the "Whig" triumphal moment, the Revolution settlement of 1688. In part 5, "The Prospect," Liberty issues her stern warning to Britain:

> On virtue can alone my kingdom stand,
> On public virtue, every virtue joined.
> For, lost this social cement of mankind,
> The greatest empires by scarce-felt degrees
> Will moulder soft away, till, tottering loose,
> They prone at last to total ruin rush.
>
> (ll. 93–98)

Liberty can maintain her reign only so long as Britons cling to independence, integrity in office, and devotion to the public good. She can be banished only by a corruption-breeding luxury:

> . . . should the broad corruptive plague
> Breathe from the city to the farthest hut
> That sits serene within the forest shade,
> The fevered people fire, inflame their wants
> And their luxurious thirst, so gathering rage
> That, were a buyer found, they stand prepared
> To sell their birthright for a cooling draught;
> Should shameless pens for plain corruption plead,
> The hired assassins of the commonweal!
>
> (ll. 317–25)

If maintained, Liberty's reign will also be blessed by "laurelled science, arts, and public works,/That lend my finished fabric comely pride,/Grandeur and grace" (ll. 375–77).

Even such a brief summary shows clearly the main theme of *Liberty:* that "public virtue" fosters and maintains freedom and that when public virtue declines, liberty is lost also. Thomson repeatedly stresses "luxury" as the villain in bringing about the degeneration of public virtue and eventual loss of liberty. Luxury is succeeded by corruption, which is in turn followed by tyranny. Thomson dramatizes and heightens the significance of the presence or absence of liberty by stressing repeatedly in the ideas and imagery several contrasting concepts: liberty–tyranny; public virtue–private interest; austerity–luxury; duty–pleasure; love–vindictiveness; benevolence-indifference; order–chaos; control–laxity; light–darkness; harmony-discord; building–destroying; growing–withering; sanity–aberration; balance–imbalance; and a number of other similar pairings. Thomson stresses particularly the necessity for active benevolence as an essential part of public virtue. This insistence on a sentimental regard for the feelings or suffering of others comes as no surprise to readers of *The Seasons*. Prominent among the native British virtues, says Thomson, is

> That Virtue known
> By the relenting look, whose equal heart
> For others feels as for another self—
> . . . .
> Whether the blameless poor, the nobly maimed,
> The lost to reason, the declined in life,
> The helpless young that kiss no mother's hand,
> And the grey second infancy of age.
>
> (IV, 486–88, 491–94)

Along with the theme of public virtue developed by Thomson largely from the example of republican Rome, he also develops in the poem a theme of "northern liberty." According to this idea, the ultimate source of British freedoms was the fierce spirit of unrestraint characteristic of the ancient Germanic or "Gothic" peoples who had swarmed over the remains of a corrupt Roman empire:

> . . . that general liberty, that soul
> Which generous nature breathes, and which, when left
> By me to bondage was corrupted Rome,
> I through the northern nations wide diffused.
> Hence many a people, fierce with freedom, rushed
> From the rude iron regions of the north,
> To Libyan deserts swarm protruding swarm,
> And poured new spirit through a slavish world.
>
> (IV, 798–805)

Hence Liberty can report that the coming of the Saxons to Britain was "the deep basis still/On which ascends my British reign" (IV,

688–89), however strengthened and refined in the course of ensuing centuries.[8]

Some of the best poetry in *Liberty* is found in passages dealing with the fine arts. Thomson was much interested in art and art criticism; he owned a great many books on art, a large number of prints of Italian Renaissance paintings, and drawings by Castelli of several famous antique statues. The extensive discussions of Greek and Renaissance art in *Liberty* form part of an oversimplified traditional scheme in which the same principles of order, harmony, and simplicity characterizing a well-governed society are shared by art produced under conditions of "liberty." In Greece, the arts depicted "heroic deeds" and "moral beauty" and thus served as "handmaids" to public virtue. The arts also provide the finishing touches, as they "lend my finished fabric comely pride,/ Grandeur and grace" (V, 376–77).

One of the few consistently praised passages of *Liberty* is Thomson's long description in part 4 of several famous antique statues, including Hercules, Meleager, the Fighting Gladiator, the Dying Gladiator, Apollo Belvedere, Flora, Venus de Medici, and Laocoon (ll. 140–206). The genuine appreciation and skill evident in these lines can be seen in the passage on Hercules:

> In leaning site, respiring from his toils,
> The well known hero who delivered Greece,
> His ample chest all tempested with force,
> Unconquerable reared. She saw the head,
> Breathing the hero, small, of Grecian size,
> Scarce more extensive than the sinewy neck;
> The spreading shoulders, muscular and broad;
> The whole a mass of swelling sinews, touched
> Into harmonious shape.
>
> (ll. 140–48)

At least two fine landscape "paintings" also appear in *Liberty*, a description of the Alps in part 4 (ll. 348–62) and another descriptive passage added to part 2 in 1738:

> There gaily broke the sun-illumined cloud;
> The lessening prospect, and the mountain blue
> Vanished in air; the precipice frowned dire;
> White down the rock the rushing torrent dashed;
> The sun shone trembling o'er the distant main;
> The tempest foamed immense; the driving storm
> Saddened the skies, and, from the doubling gloom,
> On the scathed oak the ragged lightning fell.
>
> (ll. 352–59)

These passages employ some of the techniques of painters like Claude Lorrain, Salvator Rosa, and Nicolas Poussin and are similar to a passage in *The Castle of Indolence* (I, xxxviii), which is specifically linked by Thomson to the work of Claude, Salvator, and Poussin. Elizabeth Manwaring, in her *Italian Landscapes in English Poetry* (1925), stressed the Claudian and Salvatorian influence in the landscapes of *The Seasons;* but later scholars have convincingly argued that most of *The Seasons* landscapes are patterned more upon the "heroic" or "ideal" landscapes of Renaissance and baroque art than upon the "natural" landscapes of Salvator and Claude. The "painting" passages of *Liberty* and *The Castle of Indolence* do, however, show a shift in Thomson's techniques toward the "newer" and more natural landscapes.

Thomson's celebrations of "classical" concepts of virtue, freedom, and the fine arts are accompanied in *Liberty* by a considerable amount of "Rule, Britannia" type drumbeating: "The winds and seas are Britain's wide domain,/ And not a sail but by permission spreads" (V, 636–37). *Liberty* has been called also an "Opposition" poem, meaning that a part of its purpose was to attack the Whig government under Walpole and George II. For example, the poem was dedicated in glowing terms to Prince Frederick, who became in the 1730s a willing rallying point for Tories and discontented Whigs opposed to Walpole's government. Also, Thomson's "old Whig" interpretations of English history, stern warnings about the "dangers" to liberty, and emphasis on the debilitating effects of bribery and corruption all echo themes currently being pursued in the *Craftsman*, the leading opposition newspaper. Thomson's readers in 1736 would have found sharp glances at Walpole's government in this passage:

> Should then the time arrive (which Heaven avert!)
> That Britons bend unnerved, not by the force
> Of arms, more generous and more manly, quelled,
> But by corruption's soul-dejecting arts,
> Arts impudent and gross! by their own gold,
> In part bestowed to bribe them to give all;
> With party raging, or immersed in sloth,
> Should they Britannia's well fought laurels yield
> To slily conquering Gaul, even from her brow
> Let her own naval oak be basely torn
> By such as tremble at the stiffening gale,
> And nerveless sink while others sing rejoiced;
> Or (darker prospect! scarce one gleam behind
> Disclosing) should the broad corruptive plague

Breathe from the city to the farthest hut
That sits serene within the forest shade,
The fevered people fire, inflame their wants
And their luxurious thirst, so gathering rage
That, were a buyer found, they stand prepared
To sell their birthright for a cooling draught;
Should shameless pens for plain corruption plead,
The hired assassins of the commonweal!

(V, 304–25)

On the other hand, a distinction should be made between *Liberty* and the work Thomson later did from about 1737 to 1740, when he was in the "hire" of the Opposition and overtly attacking the government. The dedication of *Liberty* to Prince Frederick in 1735 is some indication of what side Thomson was on, but not nearly as significant as a similar dedication would have been in 1738. The radical breach between Frederick and his father, after which support of the prince inevitably involved also an attack on the government, came in 1737. If the pages of the *Craftsman* are any indication, the main propaganda barrage promoting Frederick as the champion of liberty in opposition to his father and Walpole began in earnest only in late 1735. One indication of a basic change in emphasis between 1735 and 1738 is that Thomson dropped lines complimenting the king and queen (Caroline died in late 1737) from *Liberty* in 1738 and altered the wording in other passages to reflect less favorably on the king. For example, in the earlier version, the British king "invites" Liberty; in 1738, Liberty "accosts" the king, apparently without being invited (I, 364–65). The situation can perhaps be summarized by saying that, in *Liberty*, Thomson couched his dissatisfactions in terms of noble patriotic motives, with obvious implications of the shortcomings of the government, whereas a few years later he was openly attacking Walpole and the king in terms less of patriotism than of party politics and personalities. This later and much less attractive kind of "opposition" he had largely avoided in *Liberty*.

In chapter 1, I tried to explain briefly the effect of the "failure" of *Liberty* on Thomson's career and ambitions. He considered *Liberty* to be the best of his works; and the poetic career he had once visualized for himself was sidetracked permanently by the complete lack of enthusiasm with which his contemporaries received *Liberty*. In the context of a hierarchy of forms in which epic and tragedy were the highest, *Liberty* has all the trappings of a "heroic," almost "epic" performance. Both the subject matter and the expression are exalted;

the aspirations, actions, and catastrophes described are all of heroic proportions; and the use of visions, epic similes, invocations, elevated addresses, and catalogs further characterizes *Liberty* as an epic attempt. But posterity has followed the lead of Thomson's contemporaries in ignoring or condemning *Liberty.* Dr. Johnson, in a famous dictum, declared himself unable to read *Liberty;* and even those who have had the highest words of praise for *The Seasons* have typically dismissed *Liberty* with brief phrases like "dull and interminable," "series of sounding commonplaces," "gigantic failure," "Whig prize-poem," "dreary and all but unreadable." A few recent critics, however, have given some measure of praise to Thomson's lines on Greek statuary; and A. D. McKillop has admirably demonstrated the significance of *Liberty* as a "document" of Thomson's career, ideas, and milieu.

Reasons for the relative "artistic failure" of *Liberty* are not far to seek. Thomson's verse was best when his imagination operated upon visualized situations and natural emotional responses. The abstractions which are the main subject matter of *Liberty* could not be successfully visualized; and the responses, however exalted, often seem forced and artificial. Thomson did his best work when he was not straining too hard to be "noble" or "poetical." His verse can be pleasant, skillful, and natural, as in parts of *The Seasons* or *The Castle of Indolence,* and in lesser pieces like some of the "Songs" or the "Elegy on Aikman." The first version of *Winter,* one of the best things Thomson ever did, was begun "for my own amusement."[9] *The Castle of Indolence* had unpretentious beginnings in "a few detached stanzas, in the way of raillery on himself, and on some of his friends."[10] And the simple and sincere elegy for Aikman is, in Thomson's words, "rather a plain testimony of Friendship, than an attempt of poetry."[11] When he set out, on the other hand, to be deliberately "noble" or explicitly didactic, the result is the relative mediocrity of *Liberty,* the dramas, or even parts of *The Seasons.* Furthermore, the unique linguistic and stylistic qualities of Thomson's blank verse, however appropriate to *The Seasons*, proved an unfortunate vehicle for *Liberty.* His "cumulative" progression of images, heavy use of phrases and participles, and sometimes chaotic syntax had been relatively effective in capturing the sense of fulness, rapid movement, and shifts of light and color in the natural world. But a version of the same style, made even more "Miltonic" by straining for heightened effects, proved inadequate for historical narration and the explication of a complex amalgam of philosophical, political, and moral ideas taken over largely from other sources. Douglas Grant has noted of *Liberty* that "his periods are often so involved and difficult that the puzzled reader can only guess at their sense";[12] and A. D. McKillop is accurate in observing that "a systematic expository project made his blank verse harsh and labored, full of awkward inversions and choppy antitheses that strive for unwarranted emphasis and intensity."[13] Also, the problem of dealing predominantly with abstractions was met unsuccessfully by Thomson with a heavy and dull overuse of the device of personification. In *The Seasons*, he sometimes used personification to good effect in unifying his natural scenes or "as a harmonizing feature, relating man with nature, society and God."[14] In *Liberty*, however, we are subjected to too many weakly visualized series of personifications of the virtues (Courage, Justice, Labour) or tyrannical forces (Contention, Rapine, Superstition, Ignorance), unredeemed by the visualizing, organizing, or unifying functions served by some of the personifications of *The Seasons*.

II *The Tragedies*

Thomson wrote five tragedies: *Sophonisba* (1730), *Agamemnon* (1738), *Edward and Eleonora* (1739), *Tancred and Sigismunda* (1745), and *Coriolanus* (staged and published posthumously in 1749). Tragedy in general was imitative and undistinguished during the period, and Thomson was doubly unfortunate in attempting to write the pseudoclassic type of tragedy, a genre distinguished in England mainly by its "miserable paucity and poverty."[15] Although Thomson's dramatic work shows at times the mixed quality of the typical early eighteenth-century tragedy or the vague bombast of the heroic play, his aims, accomplishments, and shortcomings as a dramatist can best be understood through an examination of his attempt to write the "purely classical" or pseudoclassic tragedy. The writer of purely classical drama sought to observe the unities of time, place, and action; chose historical subjects and noble characters; wrote in a metaphorical and elevated style; utilized language rather than action to convey meaning; avoided violence on the stage; sought to teach a moral lesson, frequently one with political implications; and commonly intended the historical subject as a fable to convey instruction to his own times. The English pseudoclassic tragedies, such as John Dennis' *Appius and Virginia* (1709), Ambrose Philips' *The Distrest Mother* (1712), Addison's *Cato* (1713), Thomson's plays, and Samuel

Johnson's *Irene* (1749), were influenced by the dramatic practice of such French writers as Jean Racine and Pierre Corneille, and even more by the dramatic theories of such French neoclassical critics as René Rapin, René Le Bossu, and André Dacier.

Thomson's dramas and what we know of his dramatic theory accord reasonably well with the characteristics described above. He was keenly interested in the playhouses and was distressed at what he considered the barbarous state of the stage and the low taste of the audience. In 1726 he lamented to Aaron Hill the "Maze of incredible Impertinence, and . . . Folly" of the Italian farces, and chastised the "Persons of the first Quality" who would stoop to attend them.[16] In 1735 he expressed his opinion that the present condition of the stage was contributing only "to barbarize the Age." On the English stage, he says,

> . . . human Nature is represented in as aukward, false, and monstrous a Manner, as the human Form was in antient Gothic Sculpture and Painting. If that were all, it might be laugh'd at, and contemn'd: But since it tends, at the same time, to confound the Head, and corrupt the Heart; since Crouds grow stupid, or barbarous, as they gaze; who can consider it in that View, without feeling an honest Indignation? And what crowns the Misfortune is, that there is no Hope of its ever being otherwise: The Root of the Evil lies too deep to be pluck'd up. Was there ever an equal Absurdity heard of, among a civiliz'd People?[17]

Thomson therefore entertained an exalted conception of the place of drama in society, and he undoubtedly thought of his own classical tragedies as efforts to restore to the stage its true dignity and function. That his effort was either misguided or futile is shown by the fact that his own undistinguished dramas are, with the exception of Addison's *Cato,* the best of the group of English pseudoclassic tragedies, which, according to Allardyce Nicoll, generally never made much impression on the average body of spectators and were almost never revived.[18] Thomson typically referred to the stage as "a powerful School of humane polite Morality," "the School which forms the Manners of the Age," and "the great, the delightful School of Manners."[19] That the audience of *Sophonisba* "rose as from a moral lecture"[20] is hardly surprising.

Thomson's tragedies observe the unities of time, place, and action. In the preface to *Sophonisba* he stresses particularly the importance of "unity of design" and quotes Racine on the importance of "a simple action, supported by the violence of passions, the beauty of sentiments, and the nobleness of expression."[21] But since these plays typically never involve much, if any, action, the "violence of passions" must be conveyed almost entirely by exaggerated, declamatory speeches. Something of the character of this dialogue can be gathered from the use of more than five hundred exclamation points and nearly three hundred question marks in the first printed edition of *Sophonisba* in 1730. Typical of the attempt to express height of passion only through language is Masinissa's "Oh Gods! my fluttering heart!" (*Soph.* 17); or Agamemnon's "Where is my Life! my Love! my *Clytemnestra!*/O let me press Thee to my fluttering Soul,/That is on wing to mix itself with thine!/O thou, for whom I live, for whom I conquer,/Than Glory brighter! O my *Clytemnestra!"* (*Aga.* 16); or Attius Tullus's "My Soul, my Friend, my Soul is all on Fire!/Thirst of Revenge consumes me!" (*Corio.,* 4). One must agree with Robert Shiels, Thomson's first biographer in 1753, that this is indeed the "false pathetic," the "swelling style" which "by aiming at the sublime . . . [is] often betrayed into the bombast."[22] Many of the speeches in Thomson's plays drag on to incredible length, while the speaker agonizes, analyzes, or philosophizes over his inner conflicts or sermonizes on honor, duty, liberty, or patriotism. All this detracts significantly from the advance of "a simple action"; and Shiels again remarks appropriately: "It was his misfortune as a dramatist, that he never knew when to have done; he makes every character speak while there is any thing to be said; and during these long interviews, the action too stands still, and the story languishes."[23]

All Thomson's tragedies are explicitly didactic; furthermore, they are all primarily political dramas. Politics appears most prominently, of course, in *Agamemnon* (1738) and *Edward and Eleonora* (1739); for in these dramas Thomson is engaging in propaganda for the Opposition. But the other dramas are also primarily political, holding up the triumphs and errors of noble leaders as lessons for the British nobility. What champion of liberty to equal Sophonisba can be found in Britain? inquires the prologue to that play. "Oh may this Island practise what we preach!" exclaims the prologue to *Agamemnon.* "*Above* Ourselves *our* COUNTRY *should* be dear" is the concluding line of *Coriolanus.*

III Sophonisba *(1730)*

Sophonisba was acted at Drury Lane on February 28, 1730, and had a first run of ten nights, the final performance coming on March

17. It was never revived.[24] Ten nights were a reasonably successful run for a new tragedy, but not a remarkable one, especially if it was never later revived. John Hewitt's *Fatal Falsehood* (1734) played only four nights; but Benjamin Martyn's *Timoleon,* which preceded *Sophonisba* at Drury Lane in 1730, played fifteen times during its first season. David Mallet's *Eurydice* (1731) and *Mustapha* (1739) both played fourteen nights during their first seasons. Thomson's *Agamemnon* (1738) played nine nights; his *Coriolanus* (1749) ten. Johnson's *Irene* played nine nights in 1749. None of these tragedies ever really came alive again. The reasonably successful first run of *Sophonisba* may be partly the result of Thomson's already considerable reputation as a poet. Samuel Johnson reports that the announcement of Thomson's first play "raised such expectation that every rehearsal was dignified with a splendid audience, collected to anticipate the delight that was preparing for the public."[25] In addition, the audience for new plays was packed whenever possible; and it was reported that "*Scotchmen* with tuneful Hands and merry Feet" had insured the success of *Sophonisba.* Furthermore, it is a commonplace of dramatic history that the eighteenth century was an age, not of the author, but of the actor. Attendance at plays was probably determined as much or more by the actors as by the work being presented. In *Sophonisba*, as in his later plays, Thomson was fortunate in his cast. The famous Anne Oldfield played Sophonisba and Robert Wilkes played Masinissa. But whatever the reason for its generally good reception, the reaction was by no means unmixed. A harshly critical pamphlet, *A Criticism on The New Sophonisba*, appeared even before *Sophonisba* was published on March 12; and shortly after an even more devastating attack appeared under the ironic title, *A Defence of the New Sophonisba.* Posing as a defense of Thomson against "Tim Birch," the author of the first pamphlet, the *Defence* fills thirty pages with merciless sarcasm on Thomson's plagiarisms, bad diction, lack of plot, weak or exaggerated character portrayal, rigid adherence to the unities, inane and bombastic speeches, long-windedness, obscurity, and a general lack of sense or meaning in any aspect of the play.

Sophonisba, dedicated to Queen Caroline, tells the story of the daughter of the Carthaginian general Hasdrubal and wife of King Syphax of Numidia. Faced with delivery "into Roman chains" when her husband is defeated by Masinissa, rival king of Numidia and ally of the Roman Scipio, she calculates, in a last bid for "liberty," to marry her old sweetheart Masinissa. Masinissa falls anew a prey to her charms, and the marriage is celebrated. But Scipio brings Masinissa to his senses, and the latter sends Sophonisba a bowl of poison, which she drinks willingly:

> Rejoice, *Phoenissa!* Give me joy, my friend!
> For here is liberty! My fears are air!
> The hand of *Rome* can never touch me more!
> Hail! perfect freedom, hail!
>
> (*Soph.*, 69)

The story of Sophonisba is told in Livy and Polybius, and became a popular subject for drama, having been utilized by several Italian and French dramatists, including Corneille, and by John Marston and Nathaniel Lee in England. In Thomson's *Sophonisba*, she is, in his own words, a "public-spirited monster," willing to sacrifice herself and others to her all-consuming patriotism. Syphax is all indignation, Scipio all honor. The central character is Masinissa, who is caught in a love-honor conflict. The play is a typical "pseudoclassic" tragedy in its structure, heightened rhetoric, political implications, and didactic purpose; but there are distinct reminders here of the Restoration heroic play in such rants as "Fire! fury! hell!" (p. 46) and in the central love-honor conflict.

The play has gained a certain notoriety from the often cited parodies of the line "Oh! Sophonisba! Sophonisba! Oh!" which was immediately altered by a wit to "Oh! Jemmy Thomson! Jemmy Thomson! oh!" and by Fielding in *Tom Thumb* to "Oh! Huncamunca, Huncamunca, oh!" Actually, the line is only the most noticeable result of the attempt to suggest heights of passion by language alone, in a play which has also "Oh happy! happy! happy!" "Oh Gods! oh patience!" and "Agony! Distraction!"

IV Agamemnon *(1738)*

By the time Thomson's *Agamemnon* was acted at Drury Lane in 1738, he was solidly lodged with the Opposition, turning out propaganda to enhance the reputation of Prince Frederick at the expense of his father George II and to undermine Walpole's position as prime minister. Allegorical satires on Walpole, particularly those produced by Henry Fielding at the Little Theater in the Haymarket, led to reinforced governmental control of dramatic productions in the Stage Licensing Act, which went into effect June 21, 1737. In

1738–1739, the prince of Wales, with Pope and Lyttelton as advisers, was encouraging a stable of writers, including Thomson, David Mallet, Aaron Hill, and Henry Brooke, to turn out political tragedy. Thomas Davies recalled in 1781 that "The two poets, Thomson and Mallet, did not pretend to understand political argument, but were supposed capable of interesting the public in favour of their master's cause, by the art of working up a fable in a tragedy, and in the drawing characters, and giving them such language, as an audience could not fail properly to apply."[26]

Agamemnon, submitted to the Licenser January 14, 1738, was the first challenge to the Licensing Act, a few innocuous comedies only having been submitted for approval since its passage. Surprisingly, its performance was allowed. It was acted April 6, 1738, and had a fair run of nine nights, with the sixth and seventh nights being, understandably enough, "By Command of the Prince and Princess of Wales." It was never revived. Undoubtedly political interest contributed to its success at the time, not only on the stage but also in printed form; for an edition of 3100 copies printed April 24 sold so rapidly that a second edition was called for only four days later.[27] Davies recalled in 1781 that the play's reference to "Delegating Power to Wicked Hands," an obvious slap at George II and Walpole, was "greatly applauded."[28] Thomson was again extremely fortunate in his cast: James Quin played Agamemnon; Mary Porter, Clytemnestra; and Susannah Maria Cibber, Cassandra.

The story told is, of course, that of the triumphant return of Agamemnon from Troy only to be murdered by his wife Clytemnestra and her lover Egisthus. While the structure of the play is largely Thomson's own, he had as models the tragedies of Aeschylus and Seneca. Although Douglas Grant and others stress Thomson's "intimate knowledge" of Aeschylus as the source, actually the play is much closer to Seneca, whose *Agamemnon* Thomson owned in the 1581 English translation by John Studley.[29] Although there is little similarity of dialogue, the staging of some scenes in Thomson's play is very similar to Seneca's, such as the opening dialogue between Clytemnestra and an attendant and the ensuing scene with Clytemnestra and Egisthus. The handling of Agamemnon's death scene is similar to Seneca's, with the seer Cassandra reporting what is going on behind the scenes. Furthermore, both Seneca and Thomson compare the murder to the sacrifice of a bullock; and Thomson's "seiz'd . . .He foams in vain—Behold the lifted Blow! . . . They strike him!" (66) echoes the 1581 Studley translation: "entangled . . . He stryves in vayne. . . . shee heaves her hand to stryke. . . . He hath the stroke."[30] Thomson added the character Melisander, who has been banished to an uninhabited island by Egisthus and is picked up by Agamemnon's ship returning from Troy. The function of Seneca's character Strophilus, to whom Electra entrusts the flight and safety of Orestes, is shared in Thomson's play by two characters, Arcas and Melisander.

Despite the distortion of the story in order to provide a commentary on the English political scene, *Agamemnon* is a better play than *Sophonisba.* The rant and bombast of the former play are toned down somewhat; the characters are more complex and their motivations made more believable; Thomson utilizes the character Melisander effectively to advance the plot. But the play is still hampered by the inflated rhetoric of long speeches which could only bore the spectators. That Thomson had not mastered his craft by this time is shown also by the fact that the play originally had Agamemnon's death coming in the fourth act and contained a feeble subplot. According to Benjamin Victor, writing in 1776, the first night audience "deservedly hissed and cat-called" the two final acts; and the next morning "a club of wits, with Mr. Pope at the head of them, . . . cut, and slash'd" and put the play in more presentable form.[31]

In the political allegory, Egisthus is Walpole, Agamemnon is George II, and Clytemnestra is Queen Caroline. Egisthus-Walpole is of course the villain. The king is handled gingerly, the worst being that he "Deserves some touch of Blame" for "Delegating Power to wicked Hands" (36, 43). Queen Caroline had died November 20, 1737; thus the satire on Walpole's corrupting influence on her became rather pointless. Frequent reference is made to Agamemnon's long absence from home:

> In my own Dominions,
> I am a Stranger, *Arcas.* Ten full Years,
> Or even one Day, is Absence for a King,
> Without some mighty Reason, much too long.
>
> (37)

And to his amorous misadventures:

> . . . instead of War,
> In shameful Squabbles with his nobler Friends,
> About their Captive Females, training out,
> An amorous Revel rather than a War,
> Far from his Country, Family and Queen.
>
> (10)

The contemporary audience would have recognized the allusions to George's protracted visits to Hanover, particularly that of 1736, when his refusal to tear himself from the arms of his Hanoverian mistress, Madame Walmoden, and return to his English subjects, caused a national scandal and widespread discontent. The king normally visited Hanover every third year, and he made the usual triennial visit in 1735. Becoming enamored of Madame Walmoden, he delayed his return far beyond the usual time, then spent most of the winter and spring of 1735–1736 writing long letters to his German love, precipitately prorogued Parliament on May 20, 1736, and two days later hastened away to his new love and the child she had borne him that spring. There were "shameful Squabbles" this year in Hanover, resulting from the discovery of one Monsieur Schulemberg's ladder propped against Madame Walmoden's window one night. Despite the great public discontent over his protracted absence, the king did not actually return to England until January 14, 1737. Thomson even had at hand the convenient parallel of the raging tempest which wrecked Agamemnon's ships on his return and the hurricane in which George was caught while returning and which aroused briefly fears, and hopes, that he had been lost.

V Edward and Eleonora *(1739)*

The second Opposition challenge to the Licensing Act was Mallet's *Mustapha,* another portrait of an evil minister, allowed to be acted at Drury Lane fourteen times beginning on February 13, 1739, with two performances predictably "By Command of the Prince and Princess of Wales." Thomson contributed a prologue. Again, it is not clear just why the government did not exercise its ban. But Henry Brooke's *Gustavus Vasa,* with its corrupt minister and foreign king, finally roused the government to action; and the play was denied performance on March 18 or 19, 1739, while in rehearsal at Drury Lane. Thomson's *Edward and Eleonora,* announced for performance at Covent Garden on March 29, 1739, fell the second victim of the Licensing Act. The play was submitted to the licenser on February 23 and, after being held one month, was "forbid to be acted by the Ld. Chamberlain the 26th. March. 1738/9." Thomson and his friends professed indignation that so innocuous a performance should have been banned; and, following Brooke's example, he planned a subscription edition of 1000 fine royal copies, issued May 24, followed by a trade edition of 3500 copies the following day.[32] In fact, the political content of *Edward and Eleonora* is not nearly so great as that of *Agamemnon,* but the parallel to the contemporary scene of an earlier Prince with a weak father in the hands of ministers was obvious. Edward exclaims:

> O my deluded Father! Little Joy
> Had'st thou in Life, led from thy real Good
> And genuine Glory, from thy People's Love,
> That noblest Aim of Kings, by smiling Traitors.
> (*E. and E.,* 49)

Edward and Eleonora did eventually claim its brief turn on the stage. In 1775 Thomas Hull altered the play slightly; and it played at Covent Garden five nights that year between March 18 and May 1. The following season saw three more performances. According to Genest, *Edward and Eleonora* was also staged at Bath on February 12, 1780;[33] and the play was brought on at Drury Lane on October 22, 1796, with the distinguished players John Philip Kemble and Mrs. Siddons, who had performed *Tancred and Sigismunda* with success several times in the 1780s, in the lead roles. *Edward and Eleonora* also was played in New York in 1783, 1785, and 1797 and in Philadelphia in 1787 and 1799. This play, especially after Hull shortened some of the longer speeches and cut out the political allusions, has considerably more audience appeal than *Sophonisba* or *Agamemnon;* and it might have enjoyed a modest success on the English stage had it been performed during the author's lifetime.

Edward and Eleonora is based on the traditional story that the future Edward I, while in Palestine on the futile last Crusade about 1272, was stabbed with a poisoned dagger and would have perished had his faithful wife Eleonora not been willing to sacrifice her own life by sucking the wound. The play is not a true tragedy, for a *deus ex machina* in the form of an antidote makes possible a happy ending. Although the play is again classical in form and is plagued by inflated rhetoric and long speeches, Thomson altered his technique somewhat, putting into practice something he had realized as long ago as 1730: "I think of attempting another Tragedy, and on a story more addressed to common passions than that of Sophonisba. People now-a-days must have something like themselves, and a public-spirited monster can never concern them."[34] Pope, who was following the fortunes of the Opposition plays with interest in early 1739, wrote to Aaron Hill on February 14 that *Edward and Eleonora,* of which he had read three acts, "excels in the Pathetic" rather than the "Dignity of Sentiment, and Grandeur of Character" of Hill's own *Caesar*.[35] And Thomson achieved more genuine pathos in this play than in the earlier ones. "For the first half of the play, the nobility of the poisoned Edward and the lamentations of Eleonora are dwelt upon at length; and in the second, the feminine heroism of Eleonora, who had poisoned herself in her attempt to save her husband, and the masculine lamentations of Edward are drawn in equal detail."[36] Thomson hardly succeeded in portraying attractively the "common passions," but he did move closer to believable distresses and to characters with whom an audience could sympathize. That he borrowed one long speech from Euripides' *Alcestis,* with which his play shares the theme of a wife sacrificing herself for her husband, has been noted many times.

VI Tancred and Sigismunda *(1745)*

In *Tancred and Sigismunda* (1745), Thomson finally succeeded in writing a tragedy which appealed to eighteenth-century audiences. He was extremely fortunate to have Garrick and Susannah Maria Cibber, perhaps the most effective dramatic team of the mid-century, in the lead roles when the play opened at Drury Lane on March 18. It had a first run of only nine nights, but was revived in 1747, 1749, 1752, 1755, 1756, and thereafter almost annually until the end of the century. In the 1760s and again in the 1780s, the play was regularly staged at least once near the beginning of the Drury Lane season. It also became a standard piece at Covent Garden. During the 1783–1784 season, for example, *Tancred and Sigismunda* played at Drury Lane four times, at Covent Garden once, and at the Haymarket three times. It continued to be staged occasionally in London up to about 1820. Furthermore, *Tancred and Sigismunda* was popular on the American stage, playing numerous times in theaters in Boston, New York, Philadelphia, Baltimore, Charleston, and New Orleans between 1794 and 1823. John Howard Payne, the "Young Roscius" who aroused such admiration while storming the stages of America and England (1809–1813) before an early retirement, partly achieved his reputation in the role of Tancred, which he played frequently. On March 25, 1745, 5000 common and fifty fine copies of the play were printed,[37] the first of numerous eighteenth-century editions of the play. Furthermore, the play was routinely reprinted in such standard collections as *The British Theatre* and *The British Drama* as one of the twenty or thirty "best" English tragedies until late in the nineteenth century.

Tancred and Sigismunda has a more complicated plot than the three previous plays. Young Tancred, newly succeeded to the throne of Sicily, is thwarted in his determined love for Sigismunda by Matteo Siffredi, her father and lord high chancellor. Siffredi, in the interest of the peace of the realm, sacrifices his daughter's wishes by tricking Tancred into promising to marry a rival claimant to the throne and by insisting that his daughter marry Osmond, the lord high constable. Tragedy results when Osmond finds the still determined Tancred visiting his wife, is mortally wounded by Tancred, and stabs Sigismunda as he dies. The end finds Tancred prostrate with grief, rage, and suicidal intent with Siffredi pointing the moral to parents not to act "a tyrant's part," as he has done, with their children.

The play is again classical in form, keeping to the unities; but the violence is kept on stage. The play succeeded in acting partly because the typically long-winded dialogue was commonly cut by some 600 lines in the acted version. Thomson also still found it necessary to drag in a reference to the contemporary political scene. Pitt and Lyttelton, who after the fall of Walpole were less inclined to criticize the government, were sponsoring the play; and Benjamin Victor reported that the former "flaming Patriots," including Lyttelton, "A very remarkable new Lord of the Treasury," applauded loudly the play's appeal to previously warring factions "to quit mistakes" and support reasonable authority.[38] But there are several reasons for the play's greater success. Contemporary politics does not dominate it. Also, Thomson came closer to his ambition of giving the audience "common passions." He had moved from invoking Racine, the Italian neoclassical dramatists, and Corneille in the preface and prologue to *Sophonisba* toward the greater action and pathos of Shakespeare, Otway, and Rowe, all three of whom are invoked in the prologue to *Tancred and Sigismunda.* At least in intent, the appeal is "to your hearts," more than to an exalted patriotism or sense of honor. Douglas Grant has correctly emphasized the personal agony of Thomson's unsuccessful passion for Elizabeth Young as a factor in his more effective handling of a tragic love affair at this time.[39] For his plot, Thomson borrowed from Le Sage's *Gil Blas* a "nouvelle" entitled "Le Mariage de Vengeance," an exciting, well-told story which provided some of the action so sadly lacking in previous plays. The hero and heroine in Le Sage's story are called Enrique and Blanche; and Thomson may have borrowed his names from Robert

Wilmot's *Tancred and Gismunda,* one of the plays in Robert Dodsley's 1744 *A Select Collection of Old Plays,* to which Thomson subscribed. Thomson's play and Wilmot's tell different stories; but there are enough similarities in dialogue, technique, and situation (a young girl trying to subdue her passion in order to obey a tyrannical father; the making of the story into a lesson for tyrannical fathers) to make it at least interesting to speculate that Thomson had read Wilmot's play. The 1744 *Collection,* which also included plays of Shirley, Marlowe, Tourneur, Kyd, Ford, and others little known to the Augustans heretofore, may be partly responsible for Thomson's tentative move into the realms of a greater "intensité de passion"[40] and "from the duller realms of pseudo-classicism to the spacier realms of romantic enthusiasm."[41]

VII Coriolanus *(1749)*

The posthumous staging of Thomson's last tragedy, *Coriolanus,* on January 13, 1749, at Covent Garden, was a sentimental occasion. The prologue was a eulogy written by Lyttelton, Thomson's patron, and delivered by James Quin, who played Coriolanus. When Quin spoke the lines: "He lov'd his Friends (forgive this gushing Tear: / Alas! I feel I am no Actor here)," he actually shed tears, as did also much of the sympathetic audience. But setting sentiment aside, there is nothing remarkable about *Coriolanus,* undoubtedly Thomson's poorest play. After making fair progress with his craft through his first four tragedies, Thomson for some reason returned to many of the worst features of the pseudoclassic tragedy.

Shakespeare had told the story of Coriolanus from North's Plutarch. The story is one of the inherently dramatic legends of early Rome. Caius Marcius is haughty, daring, and brave, beloved of the patricians and hated by the plebeians. During a time of famine, feeling against him grows particularly strong as he treats the hungry mobs with proud insolence. Later, during the siege of Corioli, held by the Volsces, he distinguishes himself so greatly that he is given the title of "Coriolanus" and nominated to stand for consul. Persuaded by his friends to sue for the people's votes, he is nevertheless soon goaded into giving vent to his extreme hatred of the plebeian class and is banished from Rome. Seeking out the Volscian camp, he soon leads the Volsces to the gates of Rome. A Roman delegation suing for peace is scorned by Coriolanus; but he relents when an appeal is made by his mother and his wife. Denounced then by the Volsces, he is murdered by the Volscian general, who is jealous of his prominence.

Thomson apparently used the accounts in Livy and Dionysius of Halicarnassus more than Plutarch. Seeking unity of time and place, he also reduced the action to the Volscian camp after Coriolanus' banishment. The result is of little dramatic interest. There is little action to be pursued, so the space is filled with speeches and scenes dragged out interminably, while Coriolanus' character and motives are explored endlessly, with frequent overtones of Milton's Satan. Thomson attempts to portray Coriolanus as a tragic hero with one "Blot": "That, much provok'd,/He rais'd his vengeful Arm against his Country" (61). But the attempt flounders in too much rhetoric. After *Tancred and Sigismunda, Coriolanus* is a feeble anticlimax. It played ten nights in 1749 and was never revived. It is interesting to note, however, that a version of *Coriolanus* by Thomas Sheridan, made mostly by combining acts 1 and 2 of Shakespeare with the latter half of Thomson's play, achieved some popularity on the stage in the 1750s and 1760s. A 1789 version by John Philip Kemble, who made Coriolanus his most popular role, also retained some of Thomson's scenes. Despite its mediocrity, it is not without some significance that parts of Thomson's *Coriolanus* were still being declaimed at Drury Lane in the 1790s or in Baltimore or Philadelphia as late as the 1820s.

Robert Shiels, Thomson's first biographer, says that Thomson "only wrote for the stage, from a motive too obvious to be mentioned, and too strong to be resisted."[42] He means, of course, that dramas were profitable. And Thomson undoubtedly made a great deal of money from his plays. He received the profits of three benefit nights for each of the three tragedies staged during his lifetime; and his plays, particularly *Agamemnon* and *Edward and Eleonora,* sold in large numbers when published. But Thomson's motives went beyond money. He believed, with the theorists of his age, that the strictly classical tragedy, holding up examples of "public spirit and heroic virtues," was the noblest and most useful venture an author could engage in, next to the epic itself. Between *Sophonisba* (1730) and *Tancred and Sigismunda* (1745), Thomson gradually compromised his ideal to include the "common passions" that audiences wanted; and as a consequence he had a success in the latter play. But that he remained unconvinced is shown by his return in *Coriolanus* to the purely classical formulas again. Thomson achieved some stature in his own time as a dramatist; but, like many other eighteenth- and nineteenth-century writers, his plays would be today only a part of the lumber of the past had he not achieved prominence in other fields. Thomson's genius was not primarily dramatic; and it is for other accomplishments that he must claim his place in English literature.

VIII Britannia, Alfred, *and "Rule, Britannia"*

Other works by Thomson which are "political" in nature would include most prominently *Britannia* (1729) and *Alfred: A Masque, including "Rule, Britannia"* (1740). *Britannia* was a first tentative excursion into the camp of the opposition to Walpole. This 299 line blank verse poem is primarily a call to war against Spain. The pages of the *Craftsman,* the leading anti-Walpole journal, show from 1728 to 1730 a feverish concern with anti-British activities of Spain in the West Indies and at Gibraltar. Walpole's "peace policy" was under heavy attack by his foes. Thomson's "call to arms" was published anonymously, a fact not surprising in view of the possible recriminations by a touchy government. The printer of the *Craftsman,* for example, was "taken up" by the authorities in mid-1729 for publishing an inflammatory paper on the Spanish question. The publication of *Britannia* on January 21, 1729, was timed to coincide with the opening of Parliament. The fact that Parliament was "stormed" the same day by citizens demanding action against Spain[43] shows both the extreme topicality and the extreme heat of the issues treated in *Britannia.*

The speaker in the poem is the goddess Britannia, who is sitting on the "Sea-beat Shore" reflecting on her "degenerate Sons."[44] She begins with a passing reference to the arrival in England of Prince Frederick (December 3, 1728) and to the "future Glory" promised by his arrival; but her principal concern is soon forcefully stated:

> While, unchastis'd, the insulting *Spaniard* dares
> Infest the trading Flood, full of vain War
> Despise my Navies, and my Merchants seize;
> As, trusting to false Peace, they fearless roam
> The World of Waters wild, made, by the Toil,
> And liberal Blood of glorious Ages, mine:
> Nor bursts my sleeping thunder on their Head.
> Whence this unwonted Patience? this weak Doubt?
> This tame beseeching of rejected Peace?
> This meek Forbearance? This unnative Fear,
> To generous *Britons* never known before?
> . . . .

> Whence is it that the proud *Iberian* thus,
> In their own well-asserted Element,
> Dares rouze to Wrath the Masters of the Main?
> Who told him, that the big incumbent War
> Would not, ere this, have roll'd his trembling Ports
> In smoky Ruin?
>
> (ll. 23–33, 53–58)

The goddess then invokes the past glories of the English navy, especially the defeat of the Spanish Armada by Elizabeth's seamen and the Commonwealth period exploits of Admiral Robert Blake (ll. 62–105). She praises peace (ll. 106–46), but reminds Britons that even the easy-going, peace-loving man goes to war if sufficiently provoked (ll. 147–65). Britain has had, she says, more than sufficient provocation in Spain's threat to her sea empire:

> And what, my thoughtless Sons, should fire you more,
> Than when your well-earn'd Empire of the Deep
> The least beginning Injury receives?
> What better Cause can call your Lightning forth?
> Your Thunder wake? Your dearest Life demand?
> What better Cause, then when your Country sees
> The sly Destruction at her Vitals aim'd?
>
> (ll. 166–72)

Thomson adopts a "Rule, Britannia" tone in this middle section of *Britannia:* "And as you ride sublimely round the World,/ Make every Vessel stoop, make every State/ At once their Welfare and their Duty know" (ll. 188–90). Foreshadowings of *Liberty* also appear as the goddess calls Britain "A State, alone, where *Liberty* should live,/ In these late Times, this Evening of Mankind,/ When *Athens, Rome,* and *Carthage* are no more" (ll. 195–97) and as she warns of the encroachments of luxury: "Oh let not then waste Luxury impair/ That manly Soul of Toil" (ll. 248–49) and ". . . eat out the Heart/ Of *Liberty*" (ll. 254–55). *Britannia* ends with a direct address and a plea for action to the Parliament just opening.

Previous to *Britannia* in 1729, Thomson had indulged in patriotic sentiments, especially in early versions of *Summer* and *Spring.* But *Britannia* represents a departure from the earlier passages in two significant ways. First, what was earlier pure praise and panegyric becomes in *Britannia* something more than a little disgruntled, something very like an "Opposition" statement. Secondly, what was earlier broad, generalized patriotic statement becomes in *Britannia* highly topical and pointed political reference. These new tendencies have their culmination in Thomson's writing openly for the Opposition in the late 1730s. The main subject of *Britannia* was so topical that Thomson did not even pursue it to any extent in *Liberty* of the mid-1730s, a time when the heat of the Spanish question had temporarily abated. *Britannia* was pressed into service again in the late 1730s when the public outcry for war against Spain again reached a peak and forced Walpole into war in 1739.

The flattering reference to Prince Frederick in *Britannia* in 1729 was the opening move in an effort by Thomson to court the prince's favor, an effort exerted to one degree or another up until early 1748, when Thomson, along with his patron Lyttelton, fell from Frederick's good graces. Between 1729 and 1737, Thomson's gradual move toward open opposition coincides with the prince's own gradually worsening relations with his father and increasing development as a symbol of opposition to Walpole and George II. By late 1735, Prince Frederick was being touted heavily by the *Craftsman* as a future king who "will think Himself under an Obligation, whenever he comes to the Throne, to preserve the Liberties of our antient Constitution."[45] In 1736 Frederick was attempting to annoy his father in any way possible; and in 1737 the much publicized complete break occurred. From 1737 until Walpole's fall in 1742, any support of Frederick automatically involved an attack on the government. Thomson stated his own position boldly in mid-September, 1737, in a much reprinted poem described in chapter 1, "To His Royal Highness the Prince of Wales: An Ode on the Birth of the Princess Augusta." Through Lyttelton he was pensioned by the prince and openly served the Opposition in various projects, most notably the dramas *Agamemnon* and *Edward and Eleonora.* His last large effort for the prince's cause during this last hectic period of Walpole's power was *Alfred, A Masque* (1740), written in collaboration with his friend David Mallet, with music by Thomas Arne.

Alfred was privately produced in the garden of Frederick's residence at Clivedon on August 1–2, 1740, in honor of Princess Augusta's third birthday and of the anniversary of George I's accession on August 1, 1714. The later history of *Alfred* on the public stage, dealing mainly with performances in 1745, 1751, and 1773, has little to do with Thomson, but rather with rewritings and stagings of the piece by Arne, Mallet, and Garrick. As first written by Thomson and Mallet, *Alfred* is primarily a political tribute to Frederick and his family. The subject matter is more important than the slight plot or declamatory blank verse. Alfred was one of the "good" monarchs of British history, being played up by the Opposition during this period to imply by contrast the "badness" of George II. Edward III, Henry V, and Elizabeth were frequently invoked for the same purpose. Thomson praised Alfred, Edward, Henry, and Elizabeth in part 4 of *Liberty;* and he placed Alfred, Edward, and Henry prominently among Britain's "sons of glory" when he revised *Summer* in 1744. Other "Opposition" writers were also making use of the same names to embarrass George II. They frequently appear in the *Craftsman;* and Pope in 1737 invoked Alfred, Edward, and Henry in his cleverly ironic address to George II entitled "The First Epistle of the Second Book of Horace Imitated: To Augustus." In Johnson's *London* (1738), the glories of "Illustrious Edward," "Henry's victories," and "Alfred's golden reign" are called up in contrast to the sorry state of affairs in the present. Prince Frederick, furthermore, played the Opposition's game and ostentatiously associated himself with Alfred. He ordered for his gardens in Pall-Mall a fine statue of Alfred, to be inscribed "This Prince was the Founder of the Liberties and Commonwealth of England." He also erected a statue of Edward the Black Prince, thus also associating himself with the most famous and admired earlier prince of Wales.[46] *Alfred* was intended to reinforce the association of Frederick with Alfred and other "good" rulers, including Edward III and his son the Black Prince, both of whom appear prominently in the "vision" of England's "future" glory included in the masque. This vision of "A long line of kings,/ From . . . [Alfred] descending, glorious and renown'd" includes Edward III, Elizabeth, William III, and George I, who is described as "Good without show, above ambition great;/ Wise, equal, merciful, the friend of man!" Frederick's future reign is envisioned as the culmination of this line of glorious reigns. Frederick is described as "Sprung from that king beloved,"[47] George I. Thus Thomson and Mallet manage their tribute to the accession of the Hanoverian line while also, in a flagrantly political move, giving George II no notice at all. Thomson was also seeking the favor of Frederick's wife Augusta, princess of Wales, and had previously dedicated both *Agamemnon* and *Edward and Eleonora* to her. In the latter play, a parallel of Augusta to the earlier prince's devoted wife Eleonora is obviously intended. In *Alfred* the same implicit parallel is clearly present in a great amount of space given to Eltruda and Philippa in their roles as faithful wives, respectively, to Alfred and

Edward III. The vision of England's future glory culminates not only in the promised reign of Frederick but also in maritime supremacy, as *Alfred* ends with the singing of "Rule, Britannia" and a final vision in which "I see thy commerce, Britain, grasp the world:/All nations serve thee; every foreign flood,/Subjected, pays its tribute to the Thames."[48]

"Rule, Britannia," with lyrics by Thomson and music by Thomas Arne, is Thomson's best known work; for it has had for two hundred years a life of its own as one of the two great patriotic songs of Britain. It has been known to thousands who never heard of Thomas Arne, Thomson, or *Alfred*. Nevertheless, it had its origin as one of six songs in *Alfred* for which Arne composed music. Originally entitled simply "An Ode," it was sung near the end of *Alfred* by a "venerable bard":

AN ODE

1.

When *Britain* first, at heaven's command,
Arose from out the azure main;
This was the charter of the land,
And guardian angels sung *this* strain:
"Rule, *Britannia*, rule the waves;
Britons never will be slaves."

2.

The nations, not so blest as thee,
Must, in their turns, to tyrants fall:
While thou shalt flourish great and free,
The dread and envy of them all.
"Rule, *etc*.

3.

Still more majestic shalt thou rise,
More dreadful, from each foreign stroke:
As the loud blast that tears the skies,
Serves but to root thy native oak.
"Rule, *etc*.

4.

Thee haughty tyrants ne'er shall tame:
All their attempts to bend thee down,
Will but arrouse thy generous flame;
But work their woe, and thy renown.
"Rule, *etc*.

5.

To thee belongs the rural reign;
  Thy cities shall with commerce shine:
All thine shall be the subject main,
  And every shore it circles thine.
    "Rule, *etc.*

6.

The Muses, still with freedom found,
  Shall to thy happy coast repair:
Blest isle! with matchless beauty crown'd,
  And manly hearts to guard the fair.
    "Rule, *Britannia,* rule the waves;
    Britons never will be slaves."[49]

In "Rule, Britannia," Thomson overcame his usual long-windedness and his current involvement in narrow party politics to crystallize successfully in lyrical form his favorite themes of patriotism, liberty, and British maritime supremacy. The poem is a happier culmination than might have been expected of his involvement with "Whig panegyric" and the poetry of political propaganda. "Rule, Britannia" does, as has been noted more than once, echo specifically many of the ideas and images of *Britannia* and *Liberty*. But in the tone of its generalized and unqualified patriotism, it escapes the narrower political concerns of *Britannia, Liberty,* and *Alfred* and resembles more the patriotic exuberance of some of the earliest passages of *The Seasons*:

Happy Britannia! where the Queen of Arts,
Inspiring vigour, Liberty, abroad
Walks unconfined even to thy farthest cots,
And scatters plenty with unsparing hand.
. . . .
Island of bliss! amid the subject seas
That thunder round thy rocky coasts, set up,
At once the wonder, terror, and delight,
Of distant nations. . . .

(*Summer,* ll. 1442–45, 1595–98)

Since *Alfred* was a joint effort of Thomson and Mallet and since neither man ever specifically claimed "Rule, Britannia," attribution of authorship has never been absolutely certain. Thomson's authorship has been defended in many books and articles, but some of these discussions amount to little more than attempts to defame Mallet's character and abilities. The fact is that almost all available evidence is internal evidence: "connection in diction and thought with other works of Thomson";[50] and such evidence is usually notoriously unreliable in assigning authorship. On the other hand, the internal evidence which has in this case been accepted by many scholars as "conclusive" is unusually convincing; for it is true that all the ideas and images of "Rule, Britannia" do appear elsewhere in Thomson's poetry. I believe that Thomson wrote "Rule, Britannia"; but I am also compelled to acknowledge that no absolutely certain conclusion is possible on the basis of presently available information.

CHAPTER 4

The Castle of Indolence *and Other Poems*

OF Thomson's poems remaining to be discussed, *The Castle of Indolence* is by far the most important. But other pieces not previously treated, including "Hymn on Solitude," some of his "Songs," and several of his elegiac pieces, deserve at least brief mention. I will make no attempt, however, to mention all bits and pieces of "occasional" work in Thomson's canon.

I The Castle of Indolence

The Castle of Indolence is the best of the many eighteenth-century Spenserian imitations. Written in the nine-line stanza of *The Faerie Queene,* the poem consists of 158 stanzas arranged in two cantos of approximately equal length. Andrew Millar published the poem on May 7, 1748, only three months before Thomson's death. A second edition was published posthumously on September 22. Although not published until 1748, some stanzas of the poem were apparently written as early as the mid-1730s.[1] *The Seasons* remains Thomson's major poem, but *The Castle of Indolence* has maintained ever since its publication a deserved reputation as one of the finest eighteenth-century poems. Spenser's techniques were compatible to Thomson's fanciful and "amusive" bent; and some stanzas of *The Castle of Indolence* are as good, in a different vein, as the best passages of *The Seasons.*

Spenser's reputation was minimal but growing in the early eighteenth century. An age which established the heroic couplet as a standard and which worried about proper balance between wit and judgment had its suspicions of a poet who, in Addison's words, had

> In ancient tales amused a barbarous age;
> An age that yet uncultivate and rude,
> Where'er the poet's fancy led, pursued
> Through pathless fields, and unfrequented floods,
> To dens of dragons and enchanted woods.[2]

Spenser, like Chaucer, was commonly viewed as one of the "old" poets, whose manner of writing could be the source of amusing parody or burlesque, as in Pope's "The Alley." In spite of a growing serious interest in Spenser, this burlesque or semiburlesque quality survived to some extent in even the best of the early eighteenth-century Spenserian imitations, including Shenstone's *The Schoolmistress* (1742) and Thomson's *Castle of Indolence.* But fashionable denunciations of the "barbarity" of the poetry of earlier periods could not obscure finally the great imaginative and artistic genius of Spenser; and a "Spenserian Revival," leading up to Thomas Warton's *Observations on the Faerie Queene* (1754) and to the veneration of Spenser by the romantic poets, was clearly underway in Thomson's day. John Hughes edited Spenser's works as early as 1715; and more than thirty English Spenserian imitations were produced earlier than Thomson's *Castle of Indolence* in 1748.[3] Beginning with Matthew Prior's "Ode to the Queen" in 1706, they include most importantly Samuel Croxall's *An Original Canto of Spencer's Fairy Queen* (1713), William Thompson's *Epithalamium* (1736), Gilbert West's *Abuse of Travelling* (1739), William Shenstone's *The Schoolmistress* (1742), and Richard Owen Cambridge's *Archimage* (1742–1750).

Thomson apparently nourished a lifelong fondness for Spenser. For this we have the word of his first biographer Robert Shiels, who may be speaking from firsthand knowledge of Thomson's conversation when he says, "He is indeed the eldest born of Spenser, and he has often confessed that if he had any thing excellent in poetry, he owed it to the inspiration he first received from reading the Fairy Queen, in the very early part of his life."[4] In another context Shiels states that "Mr. *Thomson* being the best descriptive Poet in our Age has frequently own'd, that in this Respect he form'd his taste upon *Spencer.*"[5] On the other hand, there is little in Thomson's juvenile verse or later poems to bear out such statements. The juvenile verses echo contemporary writers like Addison, Pope, Gay, Blackmore, and Allan Ramsay; and the Miltonic and Virgilian models are paramount in his later work. Thomson may, however, have had the fondness for Spenser claimed by Shiels but could have been reluctant to make him a model because of the contemporary notion that Spenser was merely "amusing," a suitable model for burlesque rather than for serious work. Thomson's list of English worthies in *Summer,* present in the 1727 edition but expanded in both 1730 and 1744, does not include Spenser until 1744. This late addition of Spenser to the company of Shakespeare and Milton may indicate some shift of public attitude toward Spenser's art. *The Castle of Indolence* had its beginnings in the mid-1730s in raillery and burlesque and as it progressed assumed a more serious character. Patrick Murdoch, Thomson's friend and close associate, says of *The Castle of Indolence:* "It was, at first, little more than a few detached stanzas, in the way of raillery on himself, and on some of his friends, who would reproach him with indolence; while he thought them, at least, as indolent as himself. But he saw very soon, that the subject deserved to be treated more seriously, and in a form fitted to convey one of the most important moral lessons."[6] Thomson remained convinced that a proper imitation of Spenser should contain some element of the ludicrous; but he did make his imitation into a predominantly serious vehicle for some of his most cherished ideas and succeeded admirably in recapturing the cadences, images, and atmosphere of the best Spenserian manner.

Critics have commonly praised the dreamy atmosphere and playful burlesque portraits of canto 1, while lamenting that Thomson felt it necessary to add canto 2 with its heavy moralizing. But in the context of Thomson's beliefs about poetry, canto 2 was necessary to complete the plan. We may feel that the aesthetic qualities of canto 1 are greatly superior; but standing alone it would have been merely frivolous and would not have served to inculcate the social and moral awareness which was finally the paramount concern of poetry for Thomson and his contemporaries.

In canto 1, the first stanza establishes a theme for the entire poem, reminding us that life without toil and effort would be even worse: "Loose life, unruly Passions, and Diseases pale" (l. 9).[7] Stanzas 2–8, among the best in the poem, describe the lovely, restful setting and dreamlike atmosphere of the abode of the Wizard of Indolence. In stanzas 9–19, the Wizard sings the "Syren Melody" with which he allures pilgrims into the Castle. He promises sweet release and independence from all toil and care; and, like the devil, he can cite Scripture to his purpose. In stanzas 20–23, his hearers crowd into the Castle. A sleepy porter and page provide "Great Store of Caps, of Slippers, and of Gowns" for the ease of the guests, who then gain "sweet Oblivion of vile earthly Care" by drinking at the Fountain of

Nepenthe. The rule of behavior is the same as that of Rabelais' Abbey of Thélème: "do what you will" (stanzas 24–28). But, as they might in a dream, the "endless Numbers, swarming round" suddenly vanish,

> As when a Shepherd of the *Hebrid-Isles,*
> Plac'd far amid the melancholy Main,
> (Whether it be, lone Fancy him beguiles;
> Or that aerial Beings sometimes deign
> To stand, embodied, to our Senses plain)
> Sees on the naked Hill, or Valley low,
> The whilst in Ocean *Phoebus* dips his Wain,
> A vast Assembly moving to and fro:
> Then all at once in Air dissolves the wondrous Show.
>
> (stanzas 29–30)

Stanzas 31–32 break abruptly from this romantic reverie, as Thomson sharply reminds himself that patriotic epic and the tragic drama are worthier subjects for the Muse than dreams. Just as abruptly, however, he returns to the description of the Castle, piling up tantalizing images of touch, taste, sight, and sound to create a kind of Arabian Nights paradise (stanzas 33–42). A climax of this voluptuous reverie is reached in stanza 44, where Nature herself seems to dissolve into shadowy "Elysian Gleams" and "melting Forms." Again, Thomson abruptly breaks the mood: "No, fair Illusions! artful Phantoms, no!" Instead, he calls upon "Guardian Spirits" to visit him with visions of virtue and innocence (stanzas 45–48). In stanzas 49–56, a "Mirror of Vanity" shows various vain and foolish activities of men. Stanzas 57–72 describe various tenants of the Castle, including Thomson and some of his friends. Some of these stanzas are undoubtedly the ones first written "in the way of raillery on himself, and on some of his friends, who would reproach him with indolence."[8] In stanza 73, an abrupt turn is made: "Now must I mark the Villainy we found." An underground dungeon is revealed, "Where still our Inmates, when unpleasing grown,/ Diseas'd, and loathsome, privily were thrown." The final four stanzas (74–77) of canto 1 were written by John Armstrong and describe in burlesque terms various diseases brought on by indolence.

In canto 2, stanzas 1–4 establish the transition to the "bolder Song" of the defeat of Indolence by the Knight of Arts and Industry. The knight's parentage and upbringing are described (stanzas 5–13). As a civilizing force he travels westward, much like the Goddess of Liberty, to a final home in Britain, where he fosters science, art, commerce, and "A matchless Form of glorious Government" (stanzas 14–24). He then retires to a farm, where he enjoys rural retirement but also improves his estate and practices landscape gardening (stanzas 25–28). But in the meantime his good works have been corrupted by the Wizard of Indolence; and the knight vows to destroy "That Villain Archimage" (stanzas 29–34). He goes with his bard to the Castle, captures the Wizard, and commands the bard to address the inhabitants (stanzas 35–46). The song of the bard (stanzas 47–63), exhorting the listeners to renounce the false enchanter, is parallel and an answer to the Wizard's song in canto 1. Many heed the bard's warning and escape, but others grumble at the sudden disturbance of their happy existence (stanzas 64–66). The knight then negates the Wizard's magic and reveals the seemingly lovely scene to be foul, ugly, and blackened (stanzas 67–68). He also opens the dungeon underneath the Castle, rescues the inmates, and builds a hospital (stanzas 69–75). Those who refuse deliverance, their "scorned Day of Grace" past, are left to wander in the miserable hell which the Wizard's domain really is (stanzas 76–80). Canto 2 ends with a grotesque simile comparing the scene to a filthy herd of swine in Brentford (stanza 81).

In matter as well as manner, *The Castle of Indolence* shows a heavy reliance on Spenser. Any imitation of Spenser in Thomson's day would have made use of the Spenserian stanza (or some slight variation), the allegorical device, and obsolete words. Most would also employ some humor or burlesque and try to create something of a "fairyland" atmosphere. Thomson's poem has all of these characteristics to some extent, but his best achievement in imitating Spenser is in his manipulation of sounds, words, and images to produce rich sensuousness, soft melodic cadences, and vague, dreamy atmospheric effects:

> Was nought around but Images of Rest:
> Sleep-soothing Groves, and quiet Lawns between;
> And flowery Beds that slumbrous Influence kest,
> From Poppies breath'd; and Beds of pleasant Green,
> Where never yet was creeping Creature seen.
> Mean time unnumber'd glittering Streamlets play'd,
> And hurled ever-where their Waters sheen;
> That, as they bicker'd through the sunny Glade,
> Though restless still themselves, a lulling Murmur made.
>
> (canto 1, stanza 3)

A pleasing Land of Drowsy-hed it was:
Of Dreams that wave before the half-shut Eye;
And of gay Castles in the Clouds that pass,
For ever flushing round a Summer-Sky. . . .
(canto 1, stanza 6, ll. 1–4)

Soft Quilts on Quilts, on Carpets Carpets spread,
And Couches stretch around in seemly Band;
And endless Pillows rise to prop the Head;
So that each spacious Room was one full-swelling Bed.
(canto 1, stanza 33, ll. 6–9)

Spenser's moral concerns and especially his constant theme of the difficulty of distinguishing truth or reality from false illusions are well represented in *The Castle of Indolence.* More specifically, Thomson's presentation of the Castle and its overthrow is patterned closely on the enchantress Acrasia's Bower of Bliss and its overthrow by the Knight Guyon and the Palmer in *The Faerie Queene* (II, xii). *The Castle of Indolence,* not only in its general situation and theme but also in many of its details, echoes Spenser's Bower of Bliss passage: the false enchantress who turns men into beasts, the skillful imitation of nature by art, the net, the porter, the fountain in the court, the foul underground dungeon, the breaking of the magic spell by a knight, and the closing "hog" stanza, among others. Furthermore, Thomson also used freely other sections of *The Faerie Queene,* among them the House of Morpheus (I, i, 41), Archimago's Hermitage (I, i, 34), the Song of Phaedria (II, vi, 15–17), Merlin's looking glass (III, ii, 18–19), and the Cave of Despair (I, ix, 33 ff.). In addition to its reliance on Spenser, *The Castle of Indolence* shows also a large number of Miltonic echoes; a great deal of biblical paraphrase, parody, and allusion;[9] an obvious parallel with Rabelais' Abbey of Thélème; and probably some reliance on Spenser's own model Tasso.[10]

II *Structure and Significance*

Several more or less separate concerns are involved in *The Castle of Indolence.* Among these are (1) burlesque effects; (2) objective social and moral values; (3) the achieving of subjective dream-reverie effects by means of elaborate description and free play of imagination; (4) relatively "straight" satire; and (5) autobiographical commentary. An assessment of the total plan and effectiveness of the poem requires brief discussion of each of these and, most importantly, of their relationship to each other. First, the elements of the quaint, amusing, or burlesque were felt to be necessary in an imitation of Spenser. Thomson says in his "Advertisement" that "*This Poem being writ in the Manner of Spenser, the obsolete Words, and a Simplicity of Diction in some of the Lines, which borders on the Ludicrous, were necessary to make the Imitation more perfect.*"[11] Scattered lines in canto 1 such as "To tardy Swain no shrill-voic'd Matrons squall;/No Dogs, no Babes, no Wives, to stun your Ear" (xiv, 3–4) provide a slight burlesque coloring. The stanza (lxix) directed in raillery at Patrick Murdoch, "A little, round, fat, oily Man of God," is one of a very few burlesque stanzas. The four concluding stanzas by Armstrong rely heavily on the ludicrous, with Lethargy "Strech'd on his Back a mighty Lubbard lay,/Heaving his Sides, and snored Night and Day" or Hydropsy as an "Unwieldy Man! with Belly monstrous round." Canto 2, with its serious and noble moral purpose, has little of this burlesque vein; but it does end with an incongruously gross simile:

> Even so through *Brentford* Town, a Town of Mud,
> An Herd of bristly Swine is prick'd along;
> The filthy Beasts, that never chew the Cud,
> Still grunt, and squeak, and sing their troublous Song,
> And oft they plunge themselves the Mire among:
> But ay the ruthless Driver goads them on,
> And ay of barking Dogs the bitter Throng
> Makes them renew their unmelodious Moan;
> Ne ever find they Rest from their unresting Fone.

The moral lesson, although hinted at in canto 1, is found mostly in canto 2, where the honorable ideals of work, duty, social responsibility, and patriotism are thrown into the balance against indolence. Not only does Industry overthrow Indolence; but the theme expands to include all of Thomson's favorite noble ideas from *Liberty*, the tragedies, and *The Seasons*. As the Knight of Arts and Industry moves westward toward Britain, he merges with the figures of "Liberty" and "Public Virtue"; and the themes become very much like those of *Liberty*, *Britannia*, and even "Rule, Britannia." The Wizard of Indolence becomes a personification of the luxury and corruption which undermine public virtue and liberty. Reminiscent of *Liberty*, the bard's song not only admonishes to honorable toil, but also holds up the glorious examples of Greece and Rome. Furthermore, his exhortation stresses two of the favorite themes of *The Seasons*: that of nature's revelation of God, "By whom each Atom stirs, the Planets roll;/ Who fills, surrounds, informs, and agitates the Whole" and that of man's eternal progression "Through endless States of Being, still more near/ To Bliss approaching, and Perfection clear" (xlvii, 8–9; lxiii, 4–5).

But the reason and morality of canto 2 have never aroused as much admiration as the musing descriptive stanzas of canto 1, in which the poet stresses the easy, passive enjoyment of indolence, sense delights, nature, and art. It is here that the authentic Spenserian music, imagery, and atmosphere are fully utilized and experienced. The free play of imagination in these passages gives them a quality of dream or reverie; at their most subjective, as in stanza 44, reality gives way completely and becomes almost as disordered as a fantasy of Coleridge or Poe:

> And hither *Morpheus* sent his kindest Dreams,
> Raising a World of gayer Tinct and Grace;
> O'er which were shadowy cast Elysian Gleams,
> That play'd, in waving Lights, from Place to Place,
> And shed a roseate Smile on Nature's Face.
> Not *Titian's* Pencil e'er could so array,
> So fleece with Clouds the pure Etherial Space;
> Ne could it e'er such melting Forms display,
> As loose on flowery Beds all languishingly lay.

In addition to the burlesque, the moral, and the fanciful, some general satire is present in the Mirror of Vanity section, stanzas 49–56 of canto 1. And, finally, a number of autobiographical or semiautobiographical statements are scattered throughout the poem, as in canto 1, stanzas 31–32, 45–48, 57–59 and canto 2, stanzas 1–4, 23.

Despite this variety of concerns, the structural and thematic integrity of *The Castle of Indolence* as a moral poem can be defended up to a point. The opening stanza establishes a standard by which the false delights of the Castle are to be measured, and various other hints and statements in canto 1 prepare us for the moral of canto 2. Patricia Spacks has pointed out that Thomson makes constant use of negative statement in describing the Castle.[12] By this device, the reader is always being reminded of alternate possibilities, of the "normal" life being rejected. What kind of world would it be where "No living Wight could work, ne cared even for Play"? Or where there are "No Dogs, no Babes, no Wives"? Or where "nought but shadowy Forms" can be seen? Furthermore, neither the burlesque nor the satire are more than minor distractions from the moral purpose. On the other hand, however, there is a genuine conflict in the poem between the world of fancy and the world of moral and social norms. This dichotomy not only gives the poem a seriously flawed structure, but also points up dramatically a conflict which plagued Thomson throughout his poetic career. He was a dreamer, a lover, a genuine poet with a great gift for words and for subjective experience. Yet he spent most of his career grappling with "noble" themes of morality or patriotism with which neither his gift for language nor his vivid visual imagination was equipped to deal.

One important reason for the breakdown of structure in *The Castle of Indolence* is that Thomson was attempting to work out these conflicts while writing the poem. Several awkward autobiographical and transitional passages in canto 1 are the best proof of this. For example, the dream atmosphere of the Castle builds to a climax in stanza 30, which can only be called a romantic reverie. This exercise in pure imagination seems to leave the poet with nowhere to go. What he does is to launch abruptly into a harangue in which he chides himself to get moving with epic or tragic performances. Then, returning to his sensuous and imaginative descriptions, he reaches an even more subjective climax in stanza 44, which comes very near to the disordered quality of an opium dream. Again, he retreats abruptly: "No, fair Illusions! artful Phantoms, no!/ My Muse will not attempt your Fairy-Land." These awkward and frantic shifts can perhaps be partly understood in light of Thomson's repeated insistence on an ordered hierarchy of responses to nature (see chapter 2), ascending through sense, imagination, reason, and moral betterment. In *The Seasons*, sensation, imagination, and emotion in the presence of nature prepare the mind for the reception of rational and moral truths. In these passages of *The Castle of Indolence,* Thomson destroys his own system. Even in *The Seasons*, "description" and "reflection" are at times connected only with difficulty; here, the connection has clearly become impossible. Imagination or poetry of this sort is imagination or poetry for its own sweet sake. It is beautiful; but, for Thomson and his contemporaries, it is also dangerous. Thomson retreats from it; but it is too vividly felt and skillfully drawn a vision to be dominated and denied by simply reasserting the hierarchy of "Fancy, Reason, Virtue" (canto 2, stanza 3) and passing in review once more all the "nobler" themes of *The Seasons, Liberty,* and the tragedies. Thomson's acceptable order of perceptions is reasserted, but hardly reestablished. More than any other Thomson poem, *The Castle of Indolence* is, as Patricia Spacks has called it, "a particularly poignant record of personal conflict."[13]

III *Other Poems*

The best of Thomson's very short poems is perhaps his "Hymn on Solitude," first published in April, 1729, in James Ralph's *Miscellaneous Poems by Several Hands.* "Hymn on Solitude" is written in Miltonic tetrameter couplets and also shows a great similarity in tone, imagery, language, and structure to "Il Penseroso." The poem begins with an address to solitude:

> Hail, mildly pleasing solitude,
> Companion of the wise, and good;
> But, from whose holy, piercing eye,
> The herd of fools, and villains fly.
>
> Oh, how I love with thee to walk,
> And listen to thy whisper'd talk,
> Which innocence, and truth imparts,
> And melts the most obdurate hearts.[14]

The second section of the poem (ll. 9–24) describes various pleasing shapes in which solitude may appear: the philosopher, the shepherd, the lover, or the countess of Hertford. A third section (ll. 25–32) presents morning, noontide, and evening given over to solitude. Solitude is accompanied by a train of personified virtues: Innocence, Religion, Liberty, and the Muse Urania (ll. 34–40). The poem closes with a prayer:

> Oh, let me pierce thy secret cell!
> And in thy deep recesses dwell;
> Perhaps from Norwood's oak-clad hill,
> When meditation has her fill,
> I just may cast my careless eyes
> Where London's spiry turrets rise,
> Think of its crimes, its cares, its pain,
> Then shield me in the woods again.

"Hymn on Solitude" exists in five different extant versions and provides another good example of Thomson's constant tinkering with his poems as time went by or as new editions were prepared. The first version was written in 1725 and enclosed by Thomson in a letter to David Mallet.[15] In 1727 or 1728, the poem was revised and expanded to include a tribute to the countess of Hertford, to whom Thomson was making compliments in several different contexts during the late 1720s.[16] This second version of "Hymn on Solitude" is known from a surviving manuscript miscellany kept by Lady Hertford.[17] That Thomson was capable of improving greatly upon earlier poetic efforts can again be seen by comparing a central passage in the first version with its later form. The earliest form of this passage is

> Your's is the fragrant morning blush
> And your's the silent evening hush
> Your's the refulgent noonday gleam
> And your's ah then! the gelid stream.[18]

Thomson discarded these unremarkable lines and replaced them with a passage notable for language, imagery, and achievement of mood:

> Thine is the balmy breath of morn,
> Just as the dew-bent rose is born;
> And while Meridian fervours beat,
> Thine is the woodland dumb retreat;
> But chief, when evening scenes decay,
> And the faint landskip swims away,
> Thine is the doubtful soft decline,
> And that best hour of musing thine.

A third slightly revised version was printed in James Ralph's *Miscellaneous Poems* (1729), a fourth in Dodsley's *Collection of Poems* (1748), and a fifth, with further changes, in Thomson's posthumous *Poems on Several Occasions* in 1750. A comparison of the earliest form of the poem (1725) with the latest (1750) shows that Thomson retained, with some verbal changes, about thirty of his original forty-three lines, dropped thirteen, and added eighteen for a final total of forty-eight lines. Despite changes and improvements, the initial theme and structure of this pleasant meditative lyric remained largely intact. Thomson judged himself too harshly when he called the draft of the poem sent to Mallet "a few loose lines I compos'd in my last evening walk . . . [which] may be once worth the reading but no more."[19]

Most of Thomson's other short poems are "occasional" pieces, written on a variety of subjects. Some of these were not published during his lifetime; and those which were usually appeared in periodicals and miscellanies rather than in his "Works." Several of these shorter pieces were collected and published for the first time in the posthumous *Works* of 1750 and in *Poems on Several Occasions* in the same year. The earl of Buchan published some additional ones from manuscripts in his possession in 1792. A few others were first printed in nineteenth-century sources like William Goodhugh's *English Gentleman's Library Manual* (1827) and William Hone's *The Table Book* (1828). Small fugitive pieces continue to turn up in the twentieth century, such as "To Retirement: An Ode," first published in 1928[20] and "Ode on the Winter Solstice," first published in 1955.[21] Douglas Grant, in his 1951 biography, published for the first time not only several Thomson letters but also some new poems. Although Thomson's occasional pieces range over a variety of subjects and moods, they tend to be predominantly either love poems or elegiac tributes.

Thomson wrote several short love poems (usually called "songs" but occasionally "odes"), most of which resulted from his own personal experience. He was in love with love, and poured out his feelings in verse to "a succession of . . . ladies who charmed his susceptible heart by turn."[22] Some of these ladies remain anonymous, but two of the most important are known to have had a significant impact on Thomson's life and work. More than a dozen of his extant love poems were addressed to Elizabeth Young, who had such a devastating effect on Thomson's personal life in the early 1740s and who also figures prominently in the 1744 revisions of *The Seasons*.[23] She is addressed in these poems variously as Amanda, Eliza, or Myra. Also, at least three poems can be linked to Thomson's earlier infatuation with the countess of Hertford, to whom *Spring* was dedicated in 1728 and who probably inspired Thomson's long, semiautobiographical description of the "tortured lover" in *Spring* (ll. 1004–73).[24] Most of these "love songs" are pleasant but relatively undistinguished; and, with the possible exceptions of "Tell me, thou soul of her I love" and "For ever, Fortune, wilt thou prove," they do not add much to Thomson's stature or reputation.

Thomson was also prone to put his tributes and feelings into verse after the death of someone he admired. He incorporated some elegies and elegiac passages into *The Seasons*, such as the tribute to James Hammond added to *Winter* in 1744. The best of Thomson's separately published elegiac poems, *A Poem Sacred to the Memory of Sir Isaac Newton,* has been discussed in chapter 2. Next to the Newton poem his most ambitious elegy was *To the Memory of Lord Talbot* (1737). In this blank verse poem of 371 lines, Thomson paid fulsome tribute to the public wisdom and private virtues of a man who had risen to be lord chancellor and who also had been a generous patron to Thomson during the mid-1730s. This poem comes from approximately the same period of Thomson's career as *Liberty*; and an interesting link of the Talbot elegy with *Liberty* is the similar pattern of scientific imagery, exalting Talbot's character by comparisons with the light and power of the sun and with the brilliance of gems. Among Thomson's other elegies are some couplets written in 1725 "On the Death of His Mother," first printed by Buchan from manuscript in 1792. An "Epitaph on Miss Elizabeth Stanley" was published in 1750. Thomson's elegy for his friend William Aikman, written on the continent in 1731 or 1732, was published in part in 1750 and first printed in its entirety by Buchan in 1792. Parts of the Aikman poem, as noted in chapter 1, have a simplicity and directness rarely achieved by Thomson:

> As those we love decay, we die in part,
> String after string is severed from the heart;
> Till loosened life, at last but breathing clay,
> Without one pang is glad to fall away.[25]

CHAPTER 5

Reputation and Influence

I *Popularity of* The Seasons

PERHAPS the most remarkable thing about Thomson is the astonishing popularity of *The Seasons* in the eighteenth and nineteenth centuries. For *The Seasons* made Thomson enormously famous; the poem was probably known, loved, and quoted more than any other English poem for a hundred years after Thomson's death in 1748. Thomson was the poet of the common reader, the "people's poet": the painter of "some of the most tender beauties and delicate appearances of Nature,"[1] the sentimental lover, the moral teacher, the benevolent friend. Today's student of literature, usually introduced to Thomson as a minor "preromantic," and to *The Seasons* as one of "the mild and unexciting foothills to the Romantic mountains,"[2] is likely to be surprised that Thomson was for so long the leading "best-seller" in English literature. The great reputation and influence of *The Seasons*, which struck an increasingly responsive chord in more and more readers as Europe moved toward a climate of opinion usually designated "romanticism," would certainly also have surprised Thomson. For he apparently continued to the day of his death to consider epic and tragedy as the poet's hope of future fame and glory. Parts of this study have emphasized the frustration of Thomson's efforts to excel in more "heroic" literary forms. His principal models were Virgil, Spenser, and Milton, all of whom had climaxed their careers with works of epic stature. Thomson thus hoped to move from his early success with *The Seasons* to "nobler" accomplishments; and his contemporaries encouraged him in this ambition. His dream of literary immortality was nothing if not "classical"; to him, any lasting fame would be based on his classical tragedies, his epiclike poem *Liberty*, and perhaps also a great national epic as a climax to his career. But his five tragedies were soon largely forgotten; *Liberty*, which he himself valued above all his other works, fell dead-born from the press; and, after the failure of *Liberty,* he was too discouraged to attempt the epic which he had once been thrilled to believe he might write. His posthumous fame was fated to rest on *The Seasons* and, to a lesser extent, *The Castle of Indolence.*

The evidence for the popularity of *The Seasons* is overwhelmingly clear and can only be sampled and summarized here. Several hundred separate editions of *The Seasons* and of *Poetical Works* inclusive of *The Seasons* were called for during the 150 years after Thomson's death. On the basis of as yet incomplete evidence,[3] it can be stated that at least 174 editions of *The Seasons* were issued between 1750 and 1800; 270 editions between 1800 and 1850; and 124 editions between 1850 and 1900. The peak of demand came between 1790 and 1820, a thirty-year span in which at least 208 separate editions of *The Seasons* appeared. But demand continued strong up until about 1870, there having been, for example, at least 48 editions in the 1850s and 37 in the 1860s. After 1870, the numbers drop sharply, slowing to a trickle of eight editions in the 1890s, only five between 1900 and 1910, and practically none since. When the decline came, it was abrupt and precipitous; but up until about 1870 the public appetite for Thomson was voracious. The "common reader" of the nineteenth century, more literate and with more access to books than his eighteenth-century counterpart, took Thomson to his heart. Richard Altick, in his study of the mass reading public in the nineteenth century, concludes that *The Seasons* "seems to have penetrated where few other books did."[4] Incidentally, the continuing large nineteenth-century demand for *The Seasons* does not support the common contention that Thomson was eclipsed by the romantic poets. This assumption may well have resulted from the literary historian's assignment of Thomson to the niche of a "preparer of the way" for Wordsworth. In this scheme, his usefulness should have been exhausted when Wordsworth appeared. But Thomson continued popular; and the English romantics, despite their denunciations of Thomson's style as "vicious," "gross," and "meretricious," did not dethrone him. Thomson's throne in Scotland was eventually usurped by Burns; and such poets as Tennyson and Longfellow had absorbed much of his former audience by late in the nineteenth century. Thomson's popular reputation also declined as the reaction set in against Victorian piety and sentimentality. The twentieth century has commonly rehabilitated eighteenth-century writers disliked by the Victorians, such as Swift or Sterne, and relegated to lesser positions those whose reputations continued high in the nineteenth century, such as Addison or Thomson. In the twentieth century, neither the large middle-class reading audience nor the critics have been kind to the moralizing and sentimentalizing "people's poets." The reputations of Longfellow and other "schoolroom" poets have declined much more rapidly than did Thomson's in a comparable period after his death.

The great extent of Thomson's popularity can also be documented from the frequent testimony found in other writings, mostly from the nineteenth century. Only a few examples will be given from the large amount of material available. Percival Stockdale noted in 1793 that "no Poems have been read more generally, or with more pleasure than the *Seasons* of Thomson."[5] In 1808, the *Edinburgh Review* noted Thomson's "popularity exceeding that of all other poets, even those who are not his inferiors in genius."[6] John Wilson wrote in the 1830s that "*The Seasons* from that hour to this—then, now, and for ever—have been, are, and will be loved, and admired by all the world." In Scotland, this writer says, *The Seasons* "lies in many thousand cottages . . . , small, yellow-leaved, tatter'd, mean, miserable, calf-skin-bound, smoked, *stinking* . . . yet perused, pored, and pondered over."[7] In 1842, the *Penny Magazine* summed up the kind of reputation which Thomson had achieved: "If to be popular, in the best meaning of the word, that is, to be universally read and understood long after all temporary tastes or influences have ceased to act, be the best test of a poet's genius, then must we place the author of the 'Seasons' high indeed in the intellectual scale. His works are everywhere, and in all hands."[8] An 1855 critic remarked: "His popularity is less questionable than almost any other bard's. . . . It is more a true thing, an actual verity, real and practical; not merely a traditional pretence, not merely a hearsay renown."[9] But the tide of Thomson's popularity ebbed very swiftly in the latter decades of the nineteenth century; and in 1889 a German scholar referred to Thomson, with some exaggeration, as "a forgotten poet." Once begun, the reaction to Thomson was in some circles swift and contemptuous. Francis Thompson wrote in *The Academy* in 1897 that Thomson, despite his being "familiarly known by name," is actually "a very little poet," "a poet only by courtesy," and "a name that stands for little or nothing."[10] Lytton Strachey wrote in *The Spectator* in 1908 that "To the average reader of the present day 'The Seasons,' as a whole, is an intolerably tedious piece of work," full of "empty generalizations and academic pomposity."[11] Such judgments were not of course universal; but undeniably the flood of Thomson's popularity had slowed to a trickle. The very real "public demand" for Thomson which once prevailed is today nonexistent. A statement in the *Times Literary Supplement* in 1942 sounds less like a valid judgment than like a century-old echo: "In the second order of poetry he is the people's poet as surely as Keats is the poet's poet in the first order; and the revolving fashions and tastes of two hundred changing years have not dethroned him. Enduring popularity such as this has its own rights and defies superior argument."[12]

II *Influence*

First of all, the universal popularity of *The Seasons* for more than a century suggests an "influence" which cannot be sorted out or defined very specifically. Habits of thought, feeling, and expression inspired by *The Seasons* seeped into the foundations of an entire culture. Thomson's influence was prominent in merging with other factors to create climates of thought and feeling which determined basic attitudes about nature, science, humanitarianism, sentimentalism, the "sublime," and the quality of religious feeling. More specifically, the scope and extent of Thomson's influence can be indicated by sketching briefly his impact on (1) the reestablishment of blank verse in nondramatic poems; (2) the inception of a new "sublime" poetry; (3) eighteenth- and nineteenth-century poets who echo Thomson verbally or in use of poetic devices; (4) other areas of culture such as painting, music, politics, or education; and (5) European literature of the eighteenth century.

(1) Thomson was not the first poet in the eighteenth century to use blank verse in nondramatic poems, but the quality and popularity of *The Seasons* made him the chief influence in reestablishing its use on a large scale. Partly Miltonic, Thomson's blank verse was sufficiently different, with its "broken" character[13] and its "line-by-line progression, and cumulative participial modification in description and invocation without stress on external rhyming or grouping,"[14] to establish itself as a primary eighteenth-century model. The existence and popularity of such long blank verse poems as William Somerville's *The Chace* (1735), Edward Young's *Night Thoughts* (1742–1746), Mark Akenside's *Pleasures of Imagination* (1744), John Armstrong's *Art of Preserving Health* (1744), William Cowper's *The Task* (1785), and a host of other poems testify to the vogue of blank verse in the eighteenth century after Thomson.

(2) Thomson and some of his lesser contemporaries like David Mallet (*The Excursion,* 1728), Richard Savage (*The Wanderer,* 1729), and James Ralph (*Night,* 1728) were the pioneers of a new "sublime" strain in English poetry, adapting the "Georgic" poem to express the wonder, awe, and astonishment felt in the face of the variety, beauty, and magnificence of nature, which "enlarges and transports the soul!"[15] This "sublime" strain, of which *The Seasons* is the earliest important example, not only pervaded a whole series of descriptive-didactic blank verse nature poems, but colored most other poetry as well. William Powell Jones, in *The Rhetoric of Science,* has painstakingly documented the extensive influence of Thomson's *Seasons* on scores of scientific, descriptive, physico-theological, moral, and naturalist poems later in the century.[16] Josephine Miles, in her excellent study *Eras and Modes in English Poetry,* goes so far as to say that "Thomson built up the book of eighteenth-century verse" and that "His work was the center of a century's [sublime] mode."[17] The long persistence of close Thomsonian imitation may be illustrated by citing a few lines of James Grahame's *British Georgics* (1809), identical in matter and manner to *Winter* (ll. 96–105, 990–97):

> The long-piled mountain-snows at last dissolve,
> Bursting the roaring river's brittle bonds.
> Ponderous the fragments down the cataract shoot,
> And, buried in the boiling gulph below,
> Emerging, re-appear, then roll along,
> Tracing their height upon the half-sunk trees.
> But slower, by degrees, the obstructed wave
> Accumulated, crashing, scarcely seems
> To move, pausing at times, until, upheaved
> In masses huge, the lower sheet gives way.[18]

(3) A list of later writers who echo Thomson in one fashion or another would be very extensive. Borrowed phrases can be found in Gray, Sterne, Keats, Shelley, and Wordsworth, among others. Scholars have found more substantial influences on such authors as William Collins, whose extensive indebtedness to Thomson has been documented by Edward Ainsworth;[19] William Blake, on whom Thomson's influence was "marked and important";[20] and Alfred Tennyson, whose earliest acquaintance with poets was with Thomson,[21] and parts of whose work show a well-defined influence of the author of *The Seasons* and *The Castle of Indolence.*[22] Scottish poetry

of the eighteenth century, including that of Burns,[23] was in Thomson's debt.[24] In America, Thomson was extremely popular from about 1775 until 1850 and beyond, and a great many editions of *The Seasons* came from American presses during this period. Thomson was an American "best-seller"; and there are quotations, echoes, or mentions of Thomson in such diverse American authors as Dwight, Irving, Bryant, Emerson, Hawthorne, James, and Emily Dickinson.

(4) The far-reaching influence of Thomson can also be seen in the variety of other uses which the eighteenth and nineteenth centuries made of his work. Paramount among these influences is the impact of *The Seasons* on the visual arts. Just as Thomson had formed his own landscapes under the influence of painters like Guido Reni, Nicolas Poussin, Annibale Carracci, Claude Lorrain, and Salvator Rosa, his *Seasons* in turn provided inspiration for more than a century of illustrating and engraving, for the landscape gardeners, and for several famous painters. *The Seasons* was for many years the most illustrated poem in the language; beginning with William Kent in 1730 and running up to the end of the nineteenth century, hundreds of artists and engravers produced thousands of illustrations for *The Seasons*, many of them quite impressive. Landscape gardening came to be thought of in the eighteenth century as a third "sister art" along with poetry and painting; and Thomson was given credit for having "contributed in no small degree, both to influence and to direct the taste of men in this art."[25] Among the earlier painters who made some use of *The Seasons* were Thomas Gainsborough, Sir Joshua Reynolds, and Richard Wilson; but the two who were most inspired by Thomson are J. M. W. Turner and John Constable. Turner was fond of quoting Thomson, and among his pictures inspired by *The Seasons* are *Dunstanburgh Castle* and *The Slave Ship*. Constable accorded Thomson a prominent place in the history of landscape "painting" and frequently quoted lines from *The Seasons* as accompanying "texts" to his own paintings, including *Summer Cornfield, Salisbury Cathedral from the Meadows, Hadleigh Castle,* and *Old Sarum*. Other areas of Thomson's influence include music, political writing, and education. *The Seasons* was the inspiration for Joseph Haydn's last oratorio, *Die Jahreszeiten,* in 1801. Thomson's patriotic sentiments, in addition to the obvious example of "Rule, Britannia," were frequently recalled. For example, *The Anti-Jacobin; or, Weekly Examiner,* a conservative political paper of 1797–1798, borrowed epigraphs within the space of a few weeks from Thomson's *Sophonisba, Alfred, Edward and Eleonora,* and *The Seasons*. In the

nineteenth century, *The Seasons* was also adapted for a variety of interesting and sometimes puzzling educational purposes. It became a favorite "textbook for parsing," as in Josiah Swett's 1845 *Seasons,* with "Notes Grammatical and Explanatory, Adapting the work for use in Schools." James Boyd, in 1866, regretted that *The Seasons* was being used in schools "for no higher purpose than grammatical parsing" and prepared an edition in which "I have looked upon it as pre-eminently valuable, from the fulness and beauty of its teachings in all the prominent departments of Natural History," i.e., a science textbook.[26] Others were for making *The Seasons* a book of religious instruction especially appropriate for the young.

(5) Thomson enjoyed a very substantial reputation and vogue in Europe. His influence is best documented in Germany, France, Sweden, the Netherlands, and Russia; but *The Seasons* was also translated into several other languages, including Italian, Spanish, Danish, Hebrew, and Latin. His earliest European reputation—and perhaps also the most substantial and lasting—developed in Germany. The German poet Barthold H. Brockes was reading *The Seasons* by 1733, began to translate parts of the poem by 1740, and published a complete translation in 1745. *The Seasons* was retranslated at least ten more times, in both prose and verse, in the later eighteenth and early nineteenth centuries. Prominent among these translations were those by Ludwig Schubart in 1789 and Dietrich Soltau in 1823. A large number of editions of the German translations, not to mention several French and English editions, were published in Germany. Thomson was much discussed among literary men, and a number of writers imitated him in the "descriptive" vein, including Brockes, Christian E. von Kleist, Johann von Palthen, C. C. L. Hirshfeld, J. J. Dusch, Johann Bodmer, Christoph Wieland, and Salomo Gessner. Thomson also exerted some influence on writers of greater stature, including Klopstock, Schiller, and Goethe. Lessing was much interested in Thomson, especially the tragedies, which he helped make known in Germany by translating "Cibber's" life of Thomson and by encouraging the translating and publishing of the plays. The German interest in Thomson persisted, and aspects of his life, work, or influence were favorite topics for dissertations and monographs in the late nineteenth and early twentieth centuries.

Historians of French literature commonly stress the substantial influence of Thomson in France during the later eighteenth and early nineteenth centuries. In 1759, Marie-Jeanne de Chatillon Bontemps published the first complete French translation of *The Seasons*; and for decades after 1759 both translations and imitations were numerous. Margaret Cameron, in her book *L'Influence des Saisons de Thomson sur la Poésie Descriptive en France (1759–1810)*, counts nineteen separate French translations of *The Seasons* by 1850 and lists the names of thirty-eight French poets who were influenced by Thomson by 1811. Among these many "nature" poets are Saint-Lambert (*Les Saisons*, 1769), Roucher (*Les Mois*, 1779), and Nicolas-Germain Léonard (*Les Saisons*, 1787). Among the best translations are those by J. P. F. Deleuze (1801), J. Poulin (1802), and N. F. de Beaumont (1806). Some interpreters have found Thomson to be influential in the background of Rousseau's sentimentalism and humanitarianism. The fullest biography of Thomson is the work of a Frenchman, Léon Morel (1895). Among other national literatures influenced by Thomson are Swedish, Dutch, and Russian. His Swedish influence was extensive enough to provide Walter G. Johnson with material for a doctoral thesis in 1935. Johnson claims that "In no other foreign country did Thomson gain so many important followers as in Sweden."[27] A substantial body of eighteenth-century nature poetry in Sweden was stimulated principally by *The Seasons*; and writers of political and patriotic poetry also found models in *Liberty* and *Britannia*. The names Olof von Dalin, Hedvig Charlotta Nordenflycht, Gustaf Creutz, Gustaf Gyllenborg, and others discussed by Johnson are likely to be unfamiliar to most students of English literature; but they are significant as the early giants of a developing literary tradition, and their extensive use of Thomson provides another good example of far-reaching influence. Some Dutch translations, imitations, and influences of *The Seasons*, including Nicolaas Simon van Winter's *Jaargetijden*, have been described in B. G. Halberstadt's monograph *De Nederlandsche Vertalingen en Navolgingen van Thomson's Seasons*.[28] Finally, Thomson was one of the English writers who influenced a "sentimental" movement in Russian literature at the end of the eighteenth century. *The Seasons* first reached Russia in French and German translations, but there were Russian translations in 1798 and 1808; and the poem was also read in English. Just before and after 1800, Russian periodicals included "a large number of compositions . . . patently inspired by *The Seasons*." Among writers influenced by Thomson are Nicholas Karamzin (1766–1826), Vassily Zhukovski (1783–1852), and A. Ivanchikov.[29]

III *Critical Reputation*

The "critical" tradition of Thomson, especially that of *The Seasons*, is very extensive, beginning with the first publication of *Winter* in 1726 and continuing up to the present time. I have referred repeatedly in this study to critical attitudes toward different aspects of Thomson's work in various periods; and for the most part I can only summarize and generalize here. For a full discussion, the reader is referred to Ralph Cohen's highly detailed *The Art of Discrimination: Thomson's The Seasons and the Language of Criticism* (1964). Ann Mellard's University of Colorado master's thesis, *English Critical Opinions of James Thomson from 1726 to 1942* (1945), is also in most respects an excellent brief overview. To some extent, a high critical reputation went hand in hand with Thomson's earlier great popularity, as critics and public alike praised Thomson for "A just taste, a delicate sensibility to the beauties of nature, an overflowing benevolence, and that subdued piety which ever accompanies innocence of manners, and sound understanding."[30] Both popular and more sophisticated levels of commentary found appealing his "pious mind, amiable feelings, and accurate observation of natural objects."[31] But the usual paradox of a popular author in the hands of the critics is also noticeably present; there are divergent traditions of citing the popularity of *The Seasons*, on the one hand, to prove its excellence, and of citing the same popularity, on the other hand, to prove just the opposite. Wordsworth thought that the popularity of *The Seasons* was largely the result of "blind wonderment" rather than "genuine admiration" and added that "Wonder is the natural product of Ignorance; and as the soil was in *such good condition* at the time of the publication of the *Seasons,* the crop was doubtless abundant."[32] James Russell Lowell classified Thomson as "the inventor of cheap amusement for the million";[33] and a writer in 1842 attributed some of Thomson's popularity "to the circumstance that he is never too deep for his readers."[34] Some late nineteenth-century critics adopted the theory that Thomson had been fashionable partly because of his greatest weakness, a "stilted poetic diction" which, in the words of Lytton Strachey, "exactly fell in with the weak side of the taste of the eighteenth century."[35] With such wretched phrases, says George Saintsbury, he "baited the hook for his own days."[36]

Interestingly enough, there is more good Thomson criticism in both the eighteenth and twentieth centuries than in the interim period when his popularity both reached its peak and experienced its breakdown. The chief contributors to a significant body of later eighteenth-century Thomson criticism are Robert Shiels, Joseph Warton, John Aikin, Samuel Johnson, John More, John Scott, Robert Heron, and Percival Stockdale. Untroubled by the later supposed problem of how Thomson fit into "neoclassicism," "romanticism," or some hybrid of the two, much of this body of criticism is balanced and perceptive. Thomson's "diction" was something of a problem for critics from the beginning; and by the early nineteenth century such writers as Wordsworth, Coleridge, and Hazlitt were leading the charge at full gallop against his lack of simplicity and natural diction. These attacks, coupled with Wordsworth's assessment that "the poetry of the period intervening between the publication of the *Paradise Lost* and the *Seasons* does not contain a single new image of external nature,"[37] set in motion a long-lived critical habit of attacking Thomson's style and diction while simultaneously praising him highly for the "preromantic" feat of bringing nature back to poetry. During the nineteenth century, a fair amount of new biographical information came to light and was incorporated mainly into successive editions of Thomson in the "Aldine Poets" series by Sir Harris Nicolas, Peter Cunningham, and D. C. Tovey. In 1842, Bolton Corney published the first posthumous edition of *The Seasons* to be based on the authoritative text of 1746, a text which had eluded all previous editors and commentators. A full and detailed biography by Léon Morel came in 1895.

In the latter part of the nineteenth century, about the same time that Thomson's popular reputation was declining rapidly, the writing of "histories of English literature" for use in schools was becoming prominent. Most of these numerous histories echoed one another in praising Wordsworth and other "romantic" writers and in condemning the "elegant persiflage and optimistic generalisation"[38] of the early eighteenth century. Furthermore, these "historians" were primarily interested in discovering and establishing "movements of literature," especially for the eighteenth and nineteenth centuries. Thomson was promptly assigned—and almost embalmed in—a niche among the movements as a "preromantic" whose significance lay in faint glimmerings and crude beginnings of romanticism which could be found in his work. In this scheme, he was assumed to be a poet of "slight positive interest" but of "very great relative or historical interest." The comments of Edmund Gosse, one of the most influential of the literary historians, can be used as illustrative. *The Seasons*, says Gosse, although published in the Augustan period, "in spirit, in temper, in style, . . . has nothing whatever to do with that age, but inaugurates another, which, if we consider exactly, culminated, after a slow but direct ascent, in Wordsworth." Thomson was one of the eighteenth-century writers "who falteringly and blindly felt their way towards better things."[39] It is small wonder that Thomson lost his "positive" interest, for who would linger in the dark amid the faltering and blind groping when the full glory of the morning is available? Despite the attempts of some twentieth-century scholars to correct this false view, most of us first learned about *The Seasons* within the wickedly persistent "preromantic" frame of reference.

Although Thomson's once great popularity with the reading public has almost entirely evaporated, he has continued to be a subject of reasonably steady scholarly and critical interest in the twentieth century. Good editions of most of his work, including variorum editions of *The Seasons* for the first time, have been made available. More information about Thomson's biography continues to appear in articles and in such excellent resources as Douglas Grant's biography in 1951 or A. D. McKillop's edition of *Letters and Documents* in 1958. Although there is still unfortunately no primary bibliography of Thomson's works, several articles, particularly those of J. E. Wells, have added to our textual and bibliographical knowledge. The rediscovery in 1942 of the sale catalog of Thomson's library, still not fully explored, added another important resource for understanding his work. Numerous articles and sections of books exploring Thomson's sources, influences, and techniques have continued to appear. Some good full length studies of *The Seasons* have been published in the past thirty years, including A. D. McKillop's *The Background of Thomson's Seasons* (1942), Patricia Spacks' *The Varied God* (1959), and Ralph Cohen's *The Unfolding of The Seasons* (1970). A sometimes radical disagreement has continued to characterize critical judgments of Thomson. F. R. Leavis would banish Thomson's work to a "by-line" of eighteenth-century poetry, bearing no "serious relation to the life of its time";[40] but Josephine Miles has contended that "His work was the center of a century's mode."[41] Reuben Brower in 1968 accused Thomson of formlessness, "bald lack of transitions," and "failure to achieve philosophic ordering";[42] but in 1970 Ralph Cohen, in a determined attempt to rehabilitate Thomson to "major" status, argued in his long and detailed *The Unfolding of The Seasons* for "reconsideration" of *The Seasons* "as a major Augustan poem" and "as an important work of art."[43] The effect of Cohen's book on Thomson's stature or reputation remains to be seen. Reviewers have been complimentary to his skill as a critic; but more than one have expressed doubt as to Thomson's "rehabilitation." As C. J. Rawson comments, "What Mr. Cohen undoubtedly does is to make many details in the poem clearer, more meaningful, or more vivid. Whether he will succeed for most readers in turning the poem into something more than the attractive, faintly self-important minor work that it is usually felt to be, is more doubtful."[44]

Few English poets have ever enjoyed as great a reputation and influence as James Thomson once did. His reputation declined abruptly toward the end of the nineteenth century, although he has continued to receive much critical attention. Recent scholars have argued whether Thomson is worthy of "revival"; but I have not attempted in this study to join the argument over whether *The Seasons* is a "minor" or a "major" poem. If appreciation for Thomson is to increase, he must be read; and the reader must discover something which appeals to his own imagination, experience, or aspirations. I have tried to aid the prospective reader by clarifying some of Thomson's backgrounds, purposes, and techniques which have been obscured by time, shifts of sensibility, cultural and social change, and the misrepresentations of tendentious literary histories. Hopefully this will assist the reader toward an understanding and appreciation of Thomson's *Seasons* and some of his other work. *The Seasons* is neither dull, dated, nor insignificant. It probably will never regain its once great popularity; but if we can shift our perspectives slightly, it is still possible to appreciate Thomson for the gifted, imaginative, and articulate poet that he was. In *The Seasons,* he dealt forcefully and imaginatively with the timeless concerns of man's relationships to nature and to God. A careful reading of *The Seasons* or *The Castle of Indolence* can still, in Thomson's words, "amuse the fancy, enlighten the head, and warm the heart."

Notes and References

Preface

1. *English Literature: An Illustrated Record* (1903; reprint New York: Macmillan, 1931), III, 270.

Chapter One

1. William Howitt, *Homes and Haunts of the Most Eminent British Poets* (New York: Harper, 1875), I, 238–39.
2. Boswell, *Life of Johnson,* ed. R. W. Chapman, corrected ed. by J. D. Fleeman (London: Oxford, 1970), p. 743.
3. Douglas Grant, *James Thomson: Poet of "The Seasons"* (London: Cresset Press, 1951), pp. 1–6.
4. Patrick Murdoch, "An Account of the Life and Writings of Mr. James Thomson," in *The Works of James Thomson* (London: A. Millar, 1762), I, ii, iv; referred to hereafter as Murdoch.
5. *James Thomson (1700–1748): Letters and Documents,* ed. A. D. McKillop (Lawrence: University of Kansas Press, 1958), p. 190; referred to hereafter as *Letters and Documents.*
6. Murdoch, p. iv.
7. From Thomson's "Preface" to the second edition of *Winter* (June, 1726); reprint in *James Thomson: Poetical Works,* ed. J. Logie Robertson (London: Oxford, 1908), p. 241; referred to hereafter as *Poetical Works.*
8. Murdoch, p. iv.
9. Grant, pp. 9–10.
10. *Poetical Works,* pp. 188–89, 241.
11. Murdoch, p. ii.
12. "Life of Thomson," in *The Lives of the Poets of Great Britain and Ireland, to the Time of Dean Swift* (London, 1753), V, 190; referred to hereafter as Shiels.
13. See *Gentleman's Magazine,* n.s. 40 (October, 1853), 368.
14. *Letters and Documents,* p. 17.
15. *Gentleman's Magazine,* n.s. 40 (October, 1853), 369.
16. Murdoch, pp. iii–iv.
17. See Douglas Grant, pp. 16–17; and Sir Alexander Grant, *The Story of the University of Edinburgh* (London: Longmans, Green, 1884), I, 264
18. Shiels, p. 192.

19. See Douglas Grant, pp. 34–35; and Léon Morel, *James Thomson: Sa Vie et Ses Oeuvres* (Paris: Librairie Hachette, 1895), p. 31.
20. Alexander Grant, pp. 262–65.
21. See Herbert Drennon, "James Thomson's Contact with Newtonianism and His Interest in Natural Philosophy," *PMLA*, 49 (1934), 71.
22. Douglas Grant, p. 23.
23. Murdoch, p. iv.
24. *Letters and Documents*, p. 34.
25. Douglas Grant, p. 26.
26. See D. Nichol Smith, "Thomson and Burns," in *Eighteenth-Century English Literature: Modern Essays in Criticism* (New York: Oxford, 1959), pp. 183–84.
27. Shiels, p. 217.
28. Murdoch, p. vii.
29. *Poetical Works*, pp. 239–40.
30. See the *Gentleman's Magazine*, 87 (April, 1818), 386.
31. See "Das Newberry Manuskript von James Thomsons Jugendgedichten," *Anglia*, 23 (1901), 129–52 and "Two 18th Century 'First Works,'" *Newberry Library Bulletin*, 4 (November, 1955), 10–23.
32. *Poetical Works*, p. 487.
33. Ibid., pp. 513–14.
34. *Poetical Works*, p. 495.
35. "Two 18th Century 'First Works,'" p. 23.
36. *Plain Dealer* (London, 1724), I, 394.
37. Shiels, p. 194; see also Murdoch, pp. v–vi.
38. *Letters and Documents*, pp. 7, 12.
39. Ibid., p. 5.
40. Ibid., p. 12.
41. See Douglas Grant, pp. 91–92.
42. *Letters and Documents*, p. 16.
43. Ibid., p. 16.
44. Quoted in A. D. McKillop, *The Background of Thomson's Seasons* (1942; reprint Hamden, Connecticut: Archon Books, 1961), pp. 176–77.
45. *Letters and Documents*, p. 24.
46. *The Adventures of Ferdinand Count Fathom* (London, n.d.), I, 1–2.
47. *Letters and Documents*, p. 40.
48. Basil Williams, *The Whig Supremacy 1714–1760*, 2d ed., rev. by C. H. Stuart (Oxford: Clarendon Press, 1962), p. 10.
49. "Introduction," in *The Political Journal of George Bubb Dodington*, ed. John Carswell and L. A. Dralle (Oxford: Clarendon Press, 1965), p. ix.
50. See prose dedication to *Summer*, in *The Poems and Plays of James Thomson* (London: William Smith, 1841), p. 11; and *Poetical Works*, pp. 156, 463.
51. *Letters and Documents*, p. 59.
52. Murdoch, p. xii.

53. Ibid., p. viii.
54. Helen S. Hughes, "Thomson and the Countess of Hertford," *Modern Philology,* 25 (1928), 441.
55. *Letters and Documents,* p. 65.
56. Quoted, with permission, from a manuscript in the Yale Library.
57. See Ralph Cohen, *The Unfolding of The Seasons* (Baltimore: Johns Hopkins, 1970), p. 329.
58. *The Craftsman,* by Caleb D'Anvers (London: R. Francklin, 1731–1737).
59. *The Castle of Indolence and Other Poems,* ed. A. D. McKillop (Lawrence: University of Kansas Press, 1961), pp. 166, 170.
60. *Letters and Documents,* p. 74.
61. Quoted in Douglas Grant, pp. 77–78.
62. Quoted in *The Background of Thomson's Seasons,* p. 177.
63. *Letters and Documents,* p. 75.
64. Murdoch, p. viii.
65. *Letters and Documents,* pp. 73–74.
66. Ibid., p. 81.
67. Ibid., pp. 77–78.
68. Ibid., p. 79.
69. A. D. McKillop, *The Background of Thomson's Liberty,* Rice Institute Pamphlet, vol. 38, no. 2 (July, 1951), p. 20.
70. *Letters and Documents,* p. 78.
71. Ibid., p. 83.
72. *Poetical Works,* p. 444.
73. See a letter of November 29, 1733, from Mrs. Conduitt to Swift, in *The Correspondence of Jonathan Swift,* ed. Harold Williams (Oxford: Clarendon Press, 1965), IV, 214.
74. See *Notes and Queries,* 11 (June 2, 1855), 418–19.
75. *Letters and Documents,* p. 105.
76. Murdoch, p. x.
77. Ibid., p. xiv.
78. Canto 1, xxxi–xxxii; cited from *The Castle of Indolence and Other Poems,* p. 81.
79. Douglas Grant, pp. 156–57.
80. Cited in William Hone, *The Table Book* (London: Hunt and Clarke, 1828), II, 109–10.
81. Ibid., II, 589.
82. See Lord Hervey, *Memoirs of the Reign of George the Second, from His Accession to the Death of Queen Caroline,* ed. John Wilson Croker (London: John Murray, 1848), I, 432–33; hereafter cited as Hervey.
83. See *Gentleman's Magazine,* 8 (1738), 132.
84. Quoted from *The Political State of Great Britain,* 54 (October, 1737), 361–62.
85. Quoted in *Gentleman's Magazine,* 7 (July, 1737), 411.

86. Ibid., p. 438.
87. Basil Williams, *The Whig Supremacy,* p. 210.
88. *The Castle of Indolence and Other Poems,* p. 168.
89. *Letters and Documents,* p. 151.
90. Quoted by Helen S. Hughes, "Thomson and the Countess of Hertford," p. 464.
91. *Letters and Documents,* pp. 146–47.
92. Ibid., p. 168.
93. Ibid., p. 184.
94. Douglas Grant, p. 222.
95. Ibid., p. 201.
96. Ralph Cohen, *The Unfolding of the Seasons,* p. 329.
97. *Letters and Documents,* p. 154.
98. Cohen, p. 43.
99. Ibid., p. 162.
100. Douglas Grant, p. 237.
101. Quoted in ibid., p. 295.
102. *Letters and Documents,* p. 192.
103. Ibid., pp. 178–79.
104. Ibid., p. 181.
105. See J. E. Wells, "Thomson's *Seasons* 'Corrected and Amended,'" *Journal of English and Germanic Philology,* 42 (1943), 104–14; and Rose Mary Davis, *The Good Lord Lyttelton* (Bethlehem, Penn.: Times Publishing Company, 1939), pp. 406–10.
106. Murdoch, p. xv.
107. *Culloden Papers* (London: Cadell and Davies, 1815), pp. 306, 309–10.
108. *An Apology for the Life of George Ann Bellamy. . . ,* Written by Herself (London: Printed for the Author, 1785), II, 37.
109. Murdoch, p. xvi.

Chapter Two

1. Citations from *The Seasons* in this chapter are from *James Thomson: Poetical Works,* ed. J. Logie Robertson (London: Oxford, 1908).
2. See *The Faerie Queene* (II, xii, 63–68).
3. *Poetical Works,* p. 241.
4. *An Essay on the Writings and Genius of Pope* (London: M. Cooper, 1756), p. 30.
5. *A History of English Romanticism in the Eighteenth Century* (1899; reprint New York: Dover, 1968), p. 111.
6. Nitchie, *Vergil and the English Poets* (1919; reprint New York: AMS Press, 1966), p. 181; Nicolson, *Mountain Gloom and Mountain Glory* (1959; reprint New York: Norton, 1963), p. 358; Cohen, *The Unfolding of The Seasons* (Baltimore: Johns Hopkins, 1970), p. 3.

7. Warton, p. 37.
8. Shiels, p. 217.
9. *Newton Demands the Muse* (Princeton: Princeton University Press, 1946), p. 159.
10. *ELH,* 20 (1953), 39–76.
11. Thomson, "A Poem Sacred to the Memory of Sir Isaac Newton," in *The Castle of Indolence and Other Poems,* ed. A. D. McKillop (Lawrence: University of Kansas Press, 1961), pp. 155–56.
12. Ibid., p. 150.
13. Anthony, earl of Shaftesbury, *Characteristics,* ed. J. M. Robertson (Indianapolis: Bobbs-Merrill, 1964), II, 98.
14. See H. N. Fairchild, *Religious Trends in English Poetry: Volume I, 1700–1740* (New York: Columbia, 1939), p. 514; and John Beresford, "Introduction," in *The Seasons* (London: Nonesuch Press, 1927), p. xx.
15. See Cohen, *The Unfolding of The Seasons.*
16. "Sketch of the Life and Writings of James Thomson," in *The Seasons* (London: T. Hurst, 1802), p. iii.
17. See "A Poem Sacred to the Memory of Sir Isaac Newton," p. 154; *Poetical Works,* p. 249; and *Edward and Eleonora* (London: A. Millar, 1739), p. 7.
18. *Spectator,* no. 465. Citations of *The Spectator* are from Donald Bond's edition (Oxford: Clarendon Press, 1965).
19. *The Happy Man: Volume II, 1700–1760* (Oslo: University of Oslo, 1958), p. 252.
20. Herbert Drennon, "Newtonianism in James Thomson's Poetry," *Englische Studien,* 70 (1936), 361.
21. "A Poem Sacred to the Memory of Sir Isaac Newton," p. 152.
22. *Letters and Documents,* p. 100.
23. *Edward and Eleonora,* p. 7.
24. *The Great Chain of Being* (1936; reprint New York: Harper and Brothers, 1960), p. 183.
25. See especially Elizabeth Nitchie, *Vergil and the English Poets,* pp. 179–96; Dwight Durling, *Georgic Tradition in English Poetry* (New York: Columbia, 1935), pp. 43–58; and John Chalker, *The English Georgic* (Baltimore: Johns Hopkins, 1969), pp. 90–140.
26. Maynard Mack, *The Garden and the City* (Toronto: University of Toronto Press, 1969), p. 235.
27. Josephine Miles, *Eras and Modes in English Poetry* (Berkeley: University of California Press, 1964), p. 49.
28. McKillop, *The Background of Thomson's Seasons* (Minneapolis: University of Minnesota Press, 1942); Hamilton, *Travel and Science in Thomson's 'Seasons'* (Ph.D. diss., Yale University, 1941).
29. Shiels, p. 202; and Johnson, *Lives of the English Poets,* ed. G. B. Hill (Oxford, 1905), III, 299.
30. Aikin, "An Essay on the Plan and Character of Thomson's Seasons,"

in *The Seasons* (1778; reprint London: A. Strahan, 1799), p. xxxviii.

31. "Notes to *The Seasons* of Thomson," appended to *The Seasons* (London: A. Hamilton, 1793), unpaged.

32. *Edinburgh Review,* 7 (1806), 330–31.

33. Evans, *Tradition and Romanticism* (1940; reprint Hamden, Connecticut: Archon, 1964), p. 91; Spacks, *The Varied God* (Berkeley: University of California Press, 1959), p. 3.

34. "The Nonstructure of Augustan Verse," *Papers on Language and Literature,* 5 (1969), 235.

35. "'Logical Structure' in Eighteenth-Century Poetry," *Philological Quarterly,* 31 (1952), 334.

36. *A Preface to Eighteenth Century Poetry* (London: Oxford, 1963), p. 161.

37. *The Unfolding of The Seasons,* pp. 12, 58.

38. Ibid., p. 306.

39. Ibid., p. 86.

40. Ibid., pp. 321–22.

41. Ibid., p. 3.

42. *Characteristics,* II, 98.

43. Thorpe, p. 244.

44. "Essay, Supplementary to the Preface (1815)," in *Poetical Works,* ed. E. de Selincourt, 2d ed. (Oxford: Clarendon Press, 1952), II, 421.

45. *Lectures on the English Poets* (1818; reprint London: George Bell, 1903), p. 114.

46. J. C. Shairp, *On Poetic Interpretation of Nature* (1877; reprint Boston: Houghton Mifflin, 1889), p. 198.

47. Geoffrey Tillotson, *Augustan Poetic Diction* (London: Athlone Press, 1964), p. 56.

48. "Thomson and Burns," in *Eighteenth Century English Literature: Modern Essays in Criticism* (New York: Oxford University Press, 1959), pp. 183–84.

49. A. M. Oliver, "The Scottish Augustans," *Scottish Poetry: A Critical Survey,* ed. J. Kinsley (London: Cassell, 1955), p. 121.

50. *The Influence of Milton on English Poetry* (1922; reprint New York: Russell and Russell, 1961), p. 136.

51. Cohen, *The Unfolding of The Seasons,* p. 7.

52. See *Autumn,* l. 1356; *Winter,* l. 693; *Spring,* l. 870; *Hymn,* l. 96; *Winter,* ll. 1016, 271; *Summer,* ll. 1138, 1247.

53. See *Summer,* l. 26; *Winter,* ll. 151, 51, 55; *Autumn,* l. 5; *Winter,* l. 159; *Summer,* l. 1622; *Winter,* l. 788; *Autumn,* l. 869; *Winter,* l. 240.

54. See *Spring,* l. 82; *Autumn,* l. 350; *Spring,* ll. 568, 837, 1052; *Summer,* ll. 162, 648; *Autumn,* l. 408; *Winter,* l. 491; *Spring,* l. 98; *Summer,* l. 94.

55. See *Spring,* l. 395; *Autumn,* l. 922; *Winter,* ll. 811, 854; *Spring,* ll. 584, 594, 617, 711, 753.

56. See Tillotson, *Augustan Poetic Diction;* and John Arthos, *The*

Language of Natural Description in Eighteenth-Century Poetry (Ann Arbor: University of Michigan Press, 1949).

57. *Augustan Poetic Diction,* p. 45.
58. See *Eras and Modes in English Poetry,* pp. 2, 11, 48–77.
59. Beers, p. 111.
60. Havens, pp. 145–46.
61. *Lives of the English Poets,* III, 298.
62. Havens, p. 146.
63. *English Poetry and the English Language,* 2d ed. (New York: Russell and Russell, 1961), pp. 82–83.
64. Ian Donaldson, "Seasonal Discrimination," *Essays in Criticism,* 15 (1965), 112.
65. Bonamy Dobrée, *English Literature in the Early Eighteenth Century, 1700–1740* (Oxford: Clarendon Press, 1959), p. 494.
66. Malcolm Goldstein, *Pope and the Augustan Stage* (Stanford: Stanford University Press, 1958), p. 47.
67. Spacks, *The Varied God,* p. 181.
68. *The Background of Thomson's Seasons,* p. 170.
69. *The Poems of Alexander Pope,* ed. John Butt (New Haven: Yale University Press, 1963), p. 808.
70. *Newton Demands the Muse,* p. 51.
71. *Science and Imagination* (Ithaca, New York: Cornell University Press, 1956), pp. 233–34.

Chapter Three

1. *An Essay on the Writings and Genius of Pope,* p. 37.
2. Cited in Douglas Grant, p. 78.
3. *The Seasons* (London, 1730), pp. 215–16.
4. Ibid., p. 173.
5. *Liberty,* II, 365–66; all citations of *Liberty* are from J. Logie Robertson, ed., *James Thomson: Poetical Works* (London: Oxford University Press, 1908).
6. *Letters and Documents,* p. 98.
7. *Poetical Works,* p. 310.
8. See Samuel Kliger, "The 'Goths' in England: An Introduction to the Gothic Vogue in Eighteenth-century Aesthetic Discussion," *Modern Philology,* 43 (1945), 107–17; see also A. D. McKillop, *The Background of Thomson's Liberty,* Rice Institute Pamphlet, vol. 38, no. 2 (July 1951), pp. 74–85. This pamphlet by McKillop provides the basic information about all phases of the "background" of *Liberty.*
9. *Letters and Documents,* p. 16.
10. Murdoch, p. xiv.
11. *Letters and Documents,* p. 83.
12. Douglas Grant, p. 146.

13. *Background of Thomson's Liberty,* p. 100.

14. Ralph Cohen, *The Unfolding of The Seasons,* p. 23.

15. Allardyce Nicoll, *A History of English Drama, 1600–1900,* vol. 2, *Early Eighteenth Century Drama,* 3d ed. (Cambridge: At the University Press, 1952), p. 96.

16. *Letters and Documents,* p. 55.

17. Ibid., p. 98.

18. Nicoll, p. 85.

19. *Letters and Documents,* pp. 98, 106.

20. Samuel Johnson, *Lives of the English Poets,* III, 288.

21. All citations of Thomson's tragedies are taken from the respective first editions of *Sophonisba,* 1730; *Agamemnon,* 1738; *Edward and Eleonora,* 1739; *Tancred and Sigismunda,* 1745; and *Coriolanus,* 1749; all London: Printed for A. Millar. References are to pages.

22. Shiels, V, 210.

23. Ibid., V, 216–17.

24. Information on the staging of the plays of Thomson and others is taken mainly from *The London Stage, 1660–1800,* 11 vols. (Carbondale, Illinois: Southern Illinois University Press, 1960–1968).

25. Johnson, *Lives of the Poets,* III, 288.

26. Thomas Davies, *Memoirs of the Life of David Garrick, Esq.* (London, 1808), II, 32.

27. "Woodfall's Ledger, 1734–1747," *Notes and Queries,* 11 (June 2, 1855), 419.

28. Davies, II, 32–33.

29. See item 48 of "Second Day's Sale," in *A Catalogue of All the Genuine Houshold Furniture . . . of Mr. James Thomson* [1749].

30. "Agamemnon," in *Seneca His Tenne Tragedies,* ed. Thomas Newton (1581; reprint New York: AMS Press, Inc., 1967), II, 134.

31. Benjamin Victor, *Original Letters, Dramatic Pieces, and Poems* (London: T. Becket, 1776), I, 10–11.

32. *Notes and Queries,* 12 (September 22, 1855), 218.

33. J. Genest, *Some Account of the English Stage from the Restoration in 1660 to 1830* (Bath, 1832), VI, 162.

34. *Letters and Documents,* p. 74.

35. *The Correspondence of Alexander Pope,* ed. George Sherburn (Oxford: Clarendon Press, 1956), IV, 166.

36. Douglas Grant, pp. 190–91.

37. *Notes and Queries,* 11 (June 2, 1855), 419.

38. *Letters and Documents,* pp. 178–79.

39. Douglas Grant, pp. 237–38.

40. Morel, p. 588.

41. Nicoll, p. 94.

42. Shiels, V, 217.

43. J. E. Wells, "Thomson's *Britannia:* Issues, Attribution, Date,

Variants," *Modern Philology,* 40 (1942), 53–54.

44. *Britannia,* ll. 1–2; All citations of *Britannia* are from *The Castle of Indolence and Other Poems,* ed. A. D. McKillop (Lawrence: University of Kansas Press, 1961), pp. 166–75.

45. *The Craftsman,* September 6, 1735.

46. Ibid.

47. *Alfred, A Masque,* in *The Poems and Plays of James Thomson* (London: William Smith, 1841), pp. 162–64.

48. Ibid., p. 165.

49. *The Castle of Indolence and Other Poems,* pp. 181–82.

50. Ibid., p. 178.

Chapter Four

1. See *Letters and Documents,* p. 197.

2. *The Works of Joseph Addison,* ed. Henry Bohn (London: George Bell and Sons, 1883), I, 23.

3. See William Lyon Phelps, *The Beginnings of the English Romantic Movement* (Boston: Ginn and Company, 1893), pp. 175–76.

4. *Lives of the Poets,* V, 217.

5. *Musidorus: A Poem Sacred to the Memory of Mr. James Thomson* (London: R. Griffiths, [1748]), p. 23.

6. "Account of the Life and Writings," p. xiv.

7. All citations of *The Castle of Indolence* are from *The Castle of Indolence and Other Poems,* ed. McKillop.

8. Murdoch, p. xiv.

9. For biblical parody and Christian implications in *The Castle of Indolence,* see J. M. Aden, "Scriptural Parody in Canto I of *The Castle of Indolence,*" *Modern Language Notes,* 71 (1956), 574–77; and R. J. Griffin, "Thomson's *The Castle of Indolence,*" *Explicator,* 21, no. 4 (December, 1962), item 33.

10. For fuller discussion of Thomson's debt to Spenser and other sources, see McKillop, "Introduction," in *The Castle of Indolence and Other Poems,* pp. 1–67. For the best available criticism and explication of *The Castle of Indolence,* see McKillop's "Introduction"; Patricia Spacks, "James Thomson: The Retreat from Vision," in *The Poetry of Vision* (Cambridge: Harvard University Press, 1967), pp. 46–65; and Earl Wasserman, *Elizabethan Poetry in the Eighteenth Century* (Urbana: University of Illinois Press, 1947), pp. 110–20.

11. *The Castle of Indolence and Other Poems,* p. 68.

12. See *The Poetry of Vision,* pp. 46–65.

13. *Eighteenth-Century Poetry* (Englewood Cliffs, N.J.: Prentice-Hall, Inc., 1964), p. 141.

14. Citations of "Hymn on Solitude" are from *The Castle of Indolence and Other Poems,* ed. McKillop.

15. See *Letters and Documents*, pp. 10–11.
16. See H. H. Campbell, "Thomson and the Countess of Hertford Yet Again," *Modern Philology*, 67 (1970), 367–69.
17. See Helen S. Hughes, "Thomson and the Countess of Hertford," *Modern Philology*, 25 (1928), 439–68.
18. *Letters and Documents*, p. 11.
19. Ibid., p. 10.
20. See Hughes, "Thomson and the Countess of Hertford," pp. 459–61.
21. See Ralph M. Williams, "Thomson's 'Ode on the Winter Solstice,'" *Modern Language Notes*, 70 (1955), 256–57.
22. Douglas Grant, p. 82.
23. See H. H. Campbell, "Thomson's *Seasons*, the Countess of Hertford, and Elizabeth Young," *Texas Studies in Literature and Language*, 14 (1972), 435–44.
24. Ibid., pp. 436–37.
25. *Poetical Works*, p. 444.

Chapter Five

1. Prose dedication to *Spring*, in *The Poems and Plays of James Thomson* (London: William Smith, 1841), p. 1.
2. Ian Donaldson, "Seasonal Discrimination," *Essays in Criticism*, 15 (1965), p. 113.
3. The most complete list of editions of *The Seasons* available at present is found in Ralph Cohen, *The Art of Discrimination* (Berkeley and Los Angeles: University of California Press, 1964), pp. 472–507.
4. *The English Common Reader* (Chicago: University of Chicago Press, 1957), p. 257.
5. "Notes to *The Seasons* of Thomson," *The Seasons* (London: A. Hamilton, 1793), unpaged.
6. Vol. 12 (April, 1808), p. 80.
7. *Recreations of Christopher North* (Edinburgh: Blackwood and Sons, 1868), II, 272.
8. Vol. 11 (March, 1842), p. 113.
9. *Littell's Living Age*, 46 (1855), 346.
10. Vol. 51 (April, 1897), p. 417.
11. *The Spectator*, March 14, 1908; reprinted in *Spectatorial Essays* (New York: Harcourt, Brace & World, 1964), pp. 153, 157.
12. Saturday, December 19, 1942, p. 618.
13. See George Saintsbury, *A History of English Prosody* (1910; reprint New York: Russell and Russell, 1961), II, 480–81.
14. Josephine Miles, *Eras and Modes in English Poetry*, p. 11.
15. Thomson, *Poetical Works*, p. 241.
16. *The Rhetoric of Science* (Berkeley and Los Angeles: University of California Press, 1966), passim.
17. *Eras and Modes*, p. 63.

18. Cited in *Quarterly Review,* 3 (1810), 458.
19. *Poor Collins: His Life, His Art, and His Influence* (Ithaca: Cornell University Press, 1937), pp. 190–99.
20. Margaret R. Lowery, *Windows of the Morning* (New Haven: Yale University Press, 1940), pp. 134–56.
21. [Hallam Tennyson], *Alfred Lord Tennyson: A Memoir by His Son* (New York: Macmillan Co., 1897), I, 11.
22. See John Churton Collins, *Illustrations of Tennyson* (London: Chatto and Windus, 1891), pp. 45, 65, 112; and John Sparrow, "Tennyson and Thomson's Shorter Poems," *London Mercury,* 21 (1929–1930), pp. 428–29.
23. F. B. Snyder, "Notes on Burns and Thomson," *JEGP,* 19 (1920), 305–17.
24. See A. M. Oliver, "The Scottish Augustans," *Scottish Poetry: A Critical Survey* (London: Cassell, 1955), p. 134.
25. Archibald Alison, *Essays on the Nature and Principles of Taste* (1790), II, 103; cited in Isabel Chase, *Horace Walpole: Gardenist* (Princeton: Princeton University Press, 1943), p. 113.
26. *The Seasons,* ed. J. R. Boyd (New York: A. S. Barnes and Company, [1866]).
27. *James Thomson's Influence on Swedish Literature in the Eighteenth Century* (Urbana: The University of Illinois, 1936), p. 6.
28. Leipzig: Frankenstein and Wagner, 1923.
29. See E. J. Simmons, "English Sentimentalism in Russian Literature," *English Literature and Culture in Russia (1553–1840)* (1935; reprint New York: Octagon Books, 1964), pp. 161–74.
30. *Critical Review,* 14 (1762), 122.
31. *Quarterly Review,* 3 (1810), 457.
32. "Essay, Supplementary to the Preface (1815)," p. 420.
33. *Complete Writings of James Russell Lowell* (1891; reprint New York: AMS Press, 1966), I, 343.
34. *Penny Magazine,* 11 (1842), 113.
35. *Spectatorial Essays,* p. 157.
36. *A Short History of English Literature* (1898; reprint New York: St. Martin's Press, 1966), p. 569.
37. "Essay, Supplementary to the Preface (1815)," pp. 419–20.
38. Edmund Gosse, *English Literature: An Illustrated Record* (1903; reprint New York: Macmillan Company, 1931), III, 269.
39. Ibid., pp. 270, 273.
40. *Revaluation* (1947; reprint New York: Norton, 1963), p. 105.
41. *Eras and Modes,* p. 63.
42. "Form and Defect of Form in Eighteenth-Century Poetry: A Memorandum," *College English,* 29 (1968), 535–41.
43. p. 324.
44. *The Yearbook of English Studies,* 2 (1972), 284.

Selected Bibliography

For a much more extensive bibliography of secondary items and some of the basic primary material, see my *James Thomson (1700–1748): An Annotated Bibliography of Selected Editions and the Important Criticism.* New York: Garland Publishing, Inc., 1976. There is no primary bibliography of Thomson's works; but Ralph Cohen has published a check list of several hundred separate editions of *The Seasons* in *The Art of Discrimination* (Berkeley: University of California Press, 1964), pp. 472–507.

PRIMARY SOURCES

1. Poetry

Poetical Works. Edited by J. Logie Robertson. London: Oxford University Press, 1908.

Thomson's Seasons: Critical Edition. Edited by Otto Zippel. Berlin: Mayer and Müller, 1908.

The Castle of Indolence and Other Poems. Edited by Alan D. McKillop. Lawrence: University of Kansas Press, 1961.

The Seasons and The Castle of Indolence. Edited by James Sambrook. Oxford: Clarendon Press, 1972.

2. Drama

Works. Edited by Patrick Murdoch. London: A. Millar, 1762. The first editions of the dramas can also be used. A volume of Thomson's dramas has been announced for publication by Garland Publishing, Inc., in their *Eighteenth-Century English Drama* series.

3. Letters

BELL, A. S. "Three New Letters of James Thomson." *Notes and Queries,* 217 (October, 1972), 367–69.

Letters and Documents. Edited by Alan D. McKillop. Lawrence: University of Kansas Press, 1958.

MCKILLOP, A. D. "Two More Thomson Letters." *Modern Philology,* 60 (1962), 128–30.

SECONDARY SOURCES

1. Eighteenth-Century Biography and Criticism

AIKIN, JOHN. "An Essay on the Plan and Character of Thomson's Seasons." In *The Seasons.* 1778; reprint London: A. Strahan, 1799. Pp. xxxiii–lxiii. Stresses Thomson's importance as a "descriptive" poet.

BUCHAN, EARL OF (DAVID STUART). *Essays on the Lives and Writings of Fletcher of Saltoun and the Poet Thomson.* London: J. DeBrett, 1792. Pp. 175–280. Includes the first publication of some letters and poems by Thomson.

HERON, ROBERT. "A Critical Essay on The Seasons." In *The Seasons.* Perth: R. Morison and Son, 1793. Separately paged following p. 250, 39 pages. Discussions of Thomson's imagery.

JOHNSON, SAMUEL. "Thomson." In *Lives of the English Poets,* edited by G. B. Hill. 3 vols. Oxford: Clarendon Press, 1905. Vol. III, pp. 281–301. First issued in 1781. One of the most balanced and influential early discussions of Thomson, although Johnson relied heavily on the earlier accounts by Shiels (1753) and Murdoch (1762).

MORE, JOHN. *Strictures, Critical and Sentimental, on Thomson's Seasons.* London: Richardson and Urquhart, 1777; reprint 1970. Adulatory and effusive.

MURDOCH, PATRICK. "An Account of the Life and Writings of Mr. James Thomson." In *The Works of James Thomson.* 2 vols. London: A. Millar, 1762. Vol. I, pp. i–xx. Written by Thomson's close friend, this "Account" is the most important source of biographical information.

SCOTT, JOHN. "On Thomson's Seasons." In *Critical Essays on Some of the Poems, of several English Poets.* London: James Phillips, 1785. Pp. 295–386. On the diction of *The Seasons.*

SHIELS, ROBERT. "The Life of Thomson." In *The Lives of the Poets of Great Britain and Ireland, to the Time of Dean Swift.* 5 vols. London, 1753. Vol. V, pp. 190–218. The earliest substantial biographical and critical essay on Thomson.

STOCKDALE, PERCIVAL. "Notes to *The Seasons* of Thomson." In *The Seasons.* London: A. Hamilton, 1793. 19 unnumbered pages. Mostly concerned with refuting Johnson's strictures on Thomson.

WARTON, JOSEPH. "The *Seasons* of Thomson." In *An Essay on the Writings and Genius of Pope.* London: M. Cooper, 1756. Pp. 41–51. One of the earliest significant criticisms and appreciations of Thomson.

2. Nineteenth-Century Biography and Criticism

BAYNE, WILLIAM. *James Thomson.* Famous Scots Series. Edinburgh: Oliphant, Anderson and Ferrier, 1898. Brief biographical and critical study.

CORNEY, BOLTON. "Memorandum on the Text of The Seasons." *Gentleman's Magazine,* 169 (1841), 145–49. The final and authoritative 1746 text of *The Seasons* had been overlooked until Corney adopted it for his edition of 1842.

CUNNINGHAM, ALLAN. "Life of James Thomson, with a Critical Notice of

The Seasons, and Castle of Indolence." In *The Seasons and The Castle of Indolence*. London: Tilt and Bogue, 1841. Pp. ix–lxviii. A valuable brief biography, contributing some new information and correcting errors in earlier accounts.

GOODHUGH, WILLIAM. "Thomson." In *The English Gentleman's Library Manual*. London: W. Goodhugh, 1827. Pp. 256–94. A significant source of original information, including previously unpublished manuscript material.

HONE, WILLIAM. *The Table Book*. 2 vols. London: Hunt and Clarke, 1828. Vol. II, pp. 108–12, 378–80, 588–91. A basic source for biographical information.

MOREL, LÉON. *James Thomson: Sa Vie Et Ses Oeuvres*. Paris: Librairie Hachette, 1895. Morel's very long and detailed biography of Thomson is still useful in many respects.

NICOLAS, SIR HARRIS. "Memoir of Thomson." In *The Poetical Works of James Thomson*. Aldine Edition. London: W. Pickering, 1830. This lengthy "Memoir" was revised by Nicolas in 1847 and reprinted with revisions by Peter Cunningham in 1860. It was the most complete biography of Thomson before Morel's book in 1895.

TOVEY, D. C. "Memoir of Thomson." In *Poetical Works of James Thomson*. Aldine Edition. London: George Bell, 1897. Pp. ix–cvii. The latest version of the Aldine "Memoir"; still sensible and useful.

WILSON, JOHN. "A Few Words on Thomson." In *Recreations of Christopher North*. 2 vols. Edinburgh: William Blackwood and Sons, 1868. Vol. II, pp. 253–73. First issued in 1842. Wilson, writing in *Blackwood's Magazine* and elsewhere, was a staunch defender of Thomson against the strictures being made on him in the early nineteenth century.

3. Twentieth-Century Biography and Criticism

A. Books

ADAMS, PERCY G. "James Thomson's Luxuriant Language," in *Graces of Harmony: Alliteration, Assonance, and Consonance in Eighteenth-Century British Poetry*. Athens: University of Georgia Press, 1977. Pp. 118–135. Discusses the substantial effect which consonant and vowel echoes have on the quality of Thomson's language.

ARTHOS, JOHN. *The Language of Natural Description in Eighteenth-Century Poetry*. Ann Arbor: University of Michigan Press, 1949. The discussions of poetic diction are useful to increase understanding of Thomson's work.

CAMERON, MARGARET M. *L'Influence des Saisons de Thomson sur la Poesie Descriptive En France (1759–1810)*. Paris: H. Champion, 1927. Influence on Saint-Lambert, Roucher, and others.

CHALKER, JOHN. "Thomson's 'Seasons,'" *The English Georgic*. Baltimore: The Johns Hopkins Press, 1969, pp. 90–140. Influence of Virgil on Thomson.

COHEN, RALPH. *The Art of Discrimination: Thomson's The Seasons and the Language of Criticism.* Berkeley and Los Angeles: University of California Press, 1964. An extensive exploration of "the principles and practice of criticism" as applied to *The Seasons* for a period of 200 years. The book also includes a valuable check list of editions of *The Seasons,* the most complete list available at present.

———. *The Unfolding of The Seasons.* Baltimore: The Johns Hopkins Press, 1970. The most recent and most sophisticated full-length study of *The Seasons.* Cohen urges "its reconsideration as a major Augustan poem" and as "an important work of art."

DEANE, C. V. *Aspects of Eighteenth Century Nature Poetry.* 1935; reprint New York: Barnes and Noble, 1968. Esp. chapters 4–5. Thomson's place in the "pictorial" tradition of eighteenth-century poetry.

DOBRÉE, BONAMY. "Thomson." In *English Literature in the Early Eighteenth Century, 1700–1740.* Oxford: Clarendon Press, 1959. Pp. 475–99. A perceptive statement of what Thomson did—and did not—accomplish.

FAIRCHILD, HOXIE NEALE. *Religious Trends in English Poetry.* Vol. 1. *1700–1740, Protestantism and the Cult of Sentiment.* New York: Columbia University Press, 1939. Pp. 509–34. Excellent discussions of the religious background of *The Seasons.*

GRANT, DOUGLAS. *James Thomson: Poet of "The Seasons."* London: Cresset, 1951. The best and most readable full-length biography of Thomson. Grant discovered and printed for the first time most of Thomson's letters to Elizabeth Young, the "Amanda" of his poems.

HAGSTRUM, JEAN H. "James Thomson." In *The Sister Arts: The Tradition of Literary Pictorialism and English Poetry from Dryden to Gray.* Chicago: University of Chicago Press, 1958. Pp. 243–67. Hagstrum alters significantly older views of Thomson's relations to the traditions of painting.

HUNT, JOHN DIXON. "The Ingenious and Descriptive Thomson," in *The Figure in the Landscape: Poetry, Painting, and Gardening during the Eighteenth Century.* Baltimore: Johns Hopkins Press, 1976. Pp. 105–144. Explains the important and complex relationships between the English landscape garden and Thomson's poetic art.

JOHNSON, WALTER C. *James Thomson's Influence on Swedish Literature in the Eighteenth Century.* Urbana: University of Illinois Press, 1936. Influence on von Dalin, Nordenflycht, and others.

JONES, WILLIAM POWELL. *The Rhetoric of Science: A Study of Scientific Ideas and Imagery in Eighteenth-Century English Poetry.* Berkeley: University of California Press, 1966. This book relies heavily on discussions of Thomson and his influence on later poets.

MACAULAY, G. C. *James Thomson.* English Men of Letters Series. London: Macmillan, 1908. A good general analysis of Thomson's career and work. Some facts and dates given pertaining to Thomson's career have been corrected by more recent research.

McKillop, Alan D. *The Background of Thomson's Seasons.* Minneapolis: University of Minnesota Press, 1942. Places *The Seasons* in the context of the philosophical and literary climate in which Thomson was working and traces specific indebtedness to a large number of works on philosophy, natural science, geography, and travel.

———. *The Background of Thomson's Liberty.* Rice Institute Pamphlet, vol. 38, no. 2 (July, 1951). Full explanation of the historical, political, moral, and cultural backgrounds.

Miles, Josephine. *Eras and Modes in English Poetry.* 2d ed. Berkeley: University of California Press, 1964. Pp. 48–77. Stresses Thomson's importance as the center of a "sublime" mode in eighteenth-century poetry.

Nicolson, Marjorie Hope. *Newton Demands the Muse: Newton's Opticks and the Eighteenth Century Poets.* Princeton: Princeton University Press, 1946. Thomson is the prize exhibit in this documentation and analysis of the influence of Newton's *Opticks.*

———. *Mountain Gloom and Mountain Glory: The Development of the Aesthetics of the Infinite.* Ithaca: Cornell University Press, 1959. Includes discussions of Thomson as a "mountain" poet.

Price, Martin. "The Theatre of Nature: James Thomson." In *To the Palace of Wisdom: Studies in Order and Energy from Dryden to Blake.* New York: Doubleday, 1964. Pp. 351–61. Stresses the "movement from close observation to intense feeling" in Thomson's poetry.

Røstvig, Maren-Sofie. "James Thomson." In *The Happy Man: Studies in the Metamorphoses of a Classical Ideal; Volume II: 1700–1760.* Oslo Studies in English, no. 8. Oslo, Norway, 1958. Pp. 250–86.

Smith, David Nichol. "Thomson-Burns." In *Some Observations on Eighteenth Century Poetry.* Toronto: University of Toronto Press, 1937. Pp. 56–81. Places emphasis on Thomson's Scottish nationality as a major factor influencing the sentiments and diction of his poetry.

Spacks, Patricia Meyer. *The Varied God: A Critical Study of Thomson's The Seasons.* Berkeley: University of California Press, 1959. Stresses the change in interest from nature to man as Thomson revised *The Seasons.*

———. *The Poetry of Vision.* Cambridge: Harvard University Press, 1967. Pp. 13–65. Stimulating critical discussions of both *The Seasons* and *The Castle of Indolence.*

Tillotson, Geoffrey. *Augustan Poetic Diction.* London: Athlone Press, 1964. Sensibly explains Thomson's "poetic diction" and corrects a long tradition of misjudgments.

Wasserman, Earl R. *Elizabethan Poetry in the Eighteenth Century.* Urbana: University of Illinois Press, 1947. Pp. 110–22. Good discussion of *The Castle of Indolence.*

B. Articles

ADEN, JOHN M. "Scriptural Parody in Canto I of The Castle of Indolence." *Modern Language Notes,* 71 (1956), 574–77. Canto 1 parodies the biblical account of the Fall of Man.

CAMPBELL, HILBERT H. "Thomson and the Countess of Hertford Yet Again." *Modern Philology,* 67 (1970), 367–69. Biographical information.

DRENNON, HERBERT. "Scientific Rationalism and James Thomson's Poetic Art." *Studies in Philology,* 31 (1934), 453–71. Thomson's predominantly rationalistic and scientific outlook.

______. "Newtonianism in James Thomson's Poetry." *Englische Studien,* 70 (1936), 358–72. Thomson's reflections of Newtonian science.

FOXON, D.F. "'Oh! Sophonisba! Sophonisba! Oh!'" *Studies in Bibliography, 12 (1959), 204*–13. Variant states of the early editions of *Sophonisba.*

HAMILTON, HORACE E. "James Thomson's Seasons: Shifts in the Treatment of Popular Subject Matter." *ELH,* 15 (1948), 110–21. On Thomson's use of sensational geographical scenes, toned down in the later revisions.

HAVENS, RAYMOND D. "Primitivism and the Idea of Progress in Thomson." *Studies in Philology,* 29 (1932), 41–52. On Thomson's failure to resolve conflicting points of view in *The Seasons.*

HUGHES, HELEN SARD. "Thomson and the Countess of Hertford." *Modern Philology,* 25 (1928), 439–68. An important article, correcting Dr. Johnson's statement that Thomson had insulted the countess in 1727, thus ending their relationship.

KERN, JEAN B. "James Thomson's Revisions of *Agamemnon.*" *Philological Quarterly,* 45 (1966), 289–303. Discusses the extensive revisions made in acts 2–5 during April, 1738.

MCKILLOP, ALAN D. "The Authorship of 'A Poem to the Memory of Mr. Congreve.'" *Modern Language Notes,* 54 (1939), 599. The poem was written by Mallet, not Thomson.

______. "Two 18th Century 'First Works.'" *Newberry Library Bulletin,* 4 (1955), 10–23. On the manuscript of Thomson's juvenile poems held by the Newberry Library.

______. "Thomson and the Licensers of the Stage." *Philological Quarterly,* 37 (1958), 448–53. Thomson's *Edward and Eleonora* (1739) was forbidden performance under provisions of the Stage Licensing Act (1737).

______. "The Early History of *Alfred.*" *Philological Quarterly,* 41 (1962), 311–24. On the early performances and later rewritings by Mallet and Arne.

MOORE, C. A. "Whig Panegyric Verse, 1700–1760." *PMLA,* 41 (1926), 362–401. Whig propaganda in the work of Thomson and others.

______. "Shaftesbury and the Ethical Poets in England, 1700–1760." *PMLA,* 31 (1916), 264–325. Discusses Thomson's humanitarianism as an example of Shaftesbury's influence.

SHELDON, ESTHER K. "Sheridan's *Coriolanus:* An 18th-Century Compromise." *Shakespeare Quarterly,* 14 (1963), 153–61. Thomas Sheridan's successful play *Coriolanus* (1755) is a combination of Thomson's and Shakespeare's plays.

TAYLOR, ERIC S. "James Thomson's Library." *TLS*, June 20, 1942, p. 312. Announces the rediscovery of the sale catalog of Thomson's library.

TODD, WILLIAM B. "The Text of *The Castle of Indolence*." *English Studies*, 34 (1953), 117–21. A model bibliographical article on the early editions.

TOMPKINS, J. M. S. "'In Yonder Grave a Druid Lies.'" *Review of English Studies*, 22 (1946), 1–16. Implications of the word "druid" in Collins' elegy of Thomson.

WASSERMAN, EARL R. "Nature Moralized: The Divine Analogy in the Eighteenth Century." *ELH*, 20 (1953), 39–76. An important article setting forth reasons for the "characteristic bipartite structure" of eighteenth-century descriptive poetry, including Thomson's.

WELLS, JOHN E. "Thomson's *Britannia:* Issues, Attribution, Date, Variants." *Modern Philology*, 40 (1942), 43–56. Particularly important for Wells' discussion of the disputed date of composition.

———. "Thomson's *Seasons* 'Corrected and Amended.'" *JEGP*, 42 (1943), 104–14. Documents George Lyttelton's extensive tampering with the text of the 1750 edition. Wells also published several other excellent bibliographical articles on Thomson's work.

Index